INNOVATING FOOD FAST

INNOVATING FOOD FAST

ALEX HEIDENREICH

NEW DEGREE PRESS

INNOVATING FOOD FAST

ISBN   978-1-64137-212-1   *Paperback*

          978-1-64137-213-8   *Ebook*

CONTENTS

CHAPTER ONE

INTRODUCTION

———

That's the thing about food today: It's no longer just about being good at food. You can't have a food company that is really good at the tech and the food is bad, but you also can't have a place that has great food but doesn't know how to make it convenient for customers.[1]

—JONATHAN NEMAN, SWEETGREEN CO-CEO

* * *

1   McGrath, Maggie. "Why $200 Million Will Make Sweetgreen The Next Big Thing In Delivery (And, Yes, A Unicorn)." *Forbes.* November 13, 2018. Accessed April 07, 2019. https://www.forbes.com/sites/maggiemcgrath/2018/11/13/the-salad-unicorn-how-sweetgreens-200-million-capital-infusion-will-propel-the-chain-to-new-heights/#152ce24d3acc.

In 1954, Ray Kroc saw the early seeds of a revolution. As a traveling salesman, he walked into the McDonald brothers' hamburger location and was blown away by what he saw.

"When I saw it working that day in 1954, I felt like some latter-day Newton who'd just had an Idaho potato caromed off his skull," Kroc described. "That night in my motel room I did a lot of heavy thinking about what I'd seen during the day. Visions of McDonald's restaurants dotting crossroads all over the country paraded through my brain."[2]

And Kroc's vision has proven largely correct—except McDonalds doesn't just dot the country… it dots the world. According to the McDonald's Corporation website (as of January 2018), the chain has locations in 101 countries. More than 36,000 restaurants around the world serve 69 million people every day.[3]

The 1950s ushered in an era of fast food that was cheaper, better-tasting, and more consistent than before. McDonalds created a simplified menu, assembly line-type process and

2   Farfan, Barbara. "Quotes From McDonald's Visonary Ray Kroc About Building a Brand." *The Balance Small Business.* Accessed April 07, 2019. https://www.thebalancesmb.com/mcdonalds-ray-kroc-quotes-2892155.

3   Rosenberg, Matt. "How Many McDonald's Restaurants Operate Worldwide?" *ThoughtCo.* January 25, 2019. Accessed April 07, 2019. https://www.thoughtco.com/number-of-mcdonalds-restaurants-worldwide-1435174.

consistent supply chain delivered through franchises dotting the country. The United States, and the world, were ready for this new innovation and—quite literally—ate it up.

The resulting growth is staggering and extends beyond just McDonald's: the fast-food industry has become woven into our social being. Industry observers estimate that fast-food restaurant sales accounted for about 20 percent of the $87 billion Americans spent on food eaten away from home last year.[4]

That's $17.4 billion dollars spent on fast food.

And fast food has become integrated into our daily routines. According to a survey taken by the Newspaper Advertising Bureau in New York, the typical American visits a fast-food place about nine times a month — five times to eat there and four times to take food out.

Over a six-month period, 93 percent of all Americans over twelve years of age visit fast-food restaurants at least once. A Gallup Poll this year indicated that 45,728,000 American adults eat out daily, and 28 percent of them visit fast-food restaurants. Of all meals eaten away from home, according to

4 "Fast Food: U.S. Growth Industry." *CQ Researcher*. Accessed March 22, 2019. https://library.cqpress.com/cqresearcher/document.php?id=cqresrre1978120800.

Gallup's calculations, 24 percent of the breakfasts, 35 percent of the lunches and 18 percent of the dinners in the United States are eaten at fast-food outlets.

Ray Kroc was right: "We provide food that customers love, day after day after day. People just want more of it."

But "wanting more of it" has led to a troubling trend in the United States and the world.

* * *

$147,000,000,000.

That is the estimated cost per year that the obesity epidemic has on U.S. medical bills every year. 39.8 percent of adults in the United States were classified as obese given the 2015–16 Centers for Disease Control and Prevention survey. According to this survey, nearly 40 percent of American adults had a body mass index at 30 or above.[5] For reference, if you were five feet and six inches tall, you would have to weigh 186 pounds or more to be classified as obese. This far exceeds the recommended weight for a 5′6″ individual.

---

5   "Adult Obesity Facts | Overweight & Obesity | CDC." *Centers for Disease Control and Prevention.* Accessed April 07, 2019. https://www.cdc.gov/obesity/data/adult.html.

Since the 1950s, when Ray Kroc and McDonald's ushered in the fast-food era, Americans have become on average 26 pounds heavier. Certainly not all the blame should be foisted on the fast-food industry, but the restaurant industry in general has kept up with the growing demands for their products.

Today, the average restaurant meal is four times larger than it was in the 1950s. Take the standard fare at McDonald's then and now:[6]

- Hamburger: 3.9 oz (1950s) → 12 oz (Today)
- French Fries: 2.4 oz (1950s) → 6.7 oz (Today)
- Soda: 7 oz (1950s) → 42 oz (Today)

Our diet has radically transformed since the 1950s—as has the average American's health. "Approximately 10 percent of U.S. adults were classified as obese during the 1950s," according to the CDC.[7] The agency reported that approximately 40 percent of U.S. adults were obese; the prevalence of obesity

6   Murray, Rheana. "Fast Food Burgers Have Tripled in Size since the 1950s: CDC graphic." *Nydailynews.com*. January 10, 2019. Accessed March 22, 2019. https://www.nydailynews.com/life-style/health/fast-food-burgers-tripled-size-1950s-cdc-graphic-article-1.1083573.

7   "Adult Obesity Facts | Overweight & Obesity | CDC." *Centers for Disease Control and Prevention*. Accessed April 07, 2019. https://www.cdc.gov/obesity/data/adult.html.

among adults in the United States has more than tripled within the last six decades.[8]

This book isn't meant to foist blame on anyone, particularly as restaurants and the fast-food industry are quick to point out that they've merely responded to consumer demands and suggest it's the consumers who have asked for larger and larger portions. The fast-food industry and its leaders like McDonald's offer products like salads, have replaced fries in Happy Meals, and continue to find new ways to reach a discerning customer.

And in fact, this book isn't *just* about fast food and its impact on our health.

It's about an entire shift in our world since the 1950s: a shift that has only just begun to affect how most of us eat. Trends such as personalization, technology, demographics, and more have created a very different world than the one Ray Kroc saw when he brought those milkshake machines to the McDonald brothers.

---

8   Police, Sara. "How Much Have Obesity Rates Risen Since 1950?" *LIVESTRONG.COM.* Accessed March 22, 2019. https://www. livestrong.com/article/384722-how-much-have-obesity-rates-risen-since-1950/.

The truth here is we are seeing a unique opportunity for innovation much like what Kroc stumbled into in the 1950s. Kroc saw the opportunity to deliver food that was cheaper, better-tasting, and more consistent than before—and he took it.

Today a new crop of innovators are popping up to reimagine Kroc's visions and adapt to a changing consumer. In some senses, it's become less about only being faster, cheaper, better-tasting, and more consistent. Consumers today are looking for qualities such as:

- Healthier (looking for options that align to a changing health-conscious consumer)
- More Diverse (looking for less of the "burger and fries" fare and more unique and different combinations)
- Safer (looking for options to track sourcing of raw ingredients)
- Convenient (looking for delivery, avoiding car travel)
- Socially Conscious (looking for ways to ensure employees are paid well, environmental concerns are addressed, and values of the companies fit their aims)

Much like Kroc saw when he first walked into the McDonald brothers' stand in 1954, today's food innovators are poised to offer an entire transformation of the food industry in the next decade.

* * *

The buying power and societal mindset power that twenty-
and thirty-somethings are bringing to the market is poised
to change everything.

As Ray Kroc pointed out, "Look after the customers and the
business will take care of itself."

And a new wave of companies is targeting these emerging
customers. One such example of the power of these trends
is seen in a salad chain started by three twenty-somethings:
Sweetgreen.

Discussed further later on, Sweetgreen is a company leading
the ultra-health, quick-service movement across the nation.
While it serves healthy food, its story goes much beyond
just that. The restaurant is looking to build a food platform,
surpassing the innovation of fellow food competitors. Sweetgreen aims to match the innovation of technology companies
and other out-of-industry companies.

Rather than operating strictly as a restaurant, Sweetgreen
wants to evolve the entire food consumption process for
its customers. The restaurant plans to use its operations to

expand to various food categories and bring their unique operations closer to the consumer.[9]

Innovation here is launched on notions of consumer preferences. With the customer wanting a new way to dine, someone must deliver. Through our capitalistic society, this is what Sweetgreen plans to implement—a delivery service that directly links the company to the customer with no delivery fee.

Additionally, Sweetgreen plans to apply blockchain technology to its operations, which currently consist of cashless payments and an app and website that control roughly half of all orders.[10] Overall, the company plans to leverage advancing technology to add to its value proposition in the age of technology. It is just one company leading the innovation movement on food service.

* * *

While I fall somewhere between the millennial and Gen Z generations, I eat very differently than my parents' generation.

---

9   McGrath, Maggie. "Why $200 Million Will Make Sweetgreen The Next Big Thing In Delivery (And, Yes, A Unicorn)." *Forbes.* November 13, 2018. Accessed April 07, 2019. https://www.forbes.com/sites/maggiemcgrath/2018/11/13/the-salad-unicorn-how-sweetgreens-200-million-capital-infusion-will-propel-the-chain-to-new-heights/#152ce24d3acc.

10   Ibid

And the wave of younger generations—us of the avocado toast, kale, and superfood champions—is only getting started.

But things weren't always this way for me.

Starting from an early age, I was overweight. I went through my elementary and middle school years being far above the weight I should have been. I grew up as an overweight child. I was allergic to what felt like everything, I had bad asthma, and I was embarrassed. My health was not where it needed to be.

During this time, I was involved in sports. I played soccer, baseball, and basketball; I learned to swim, and I was decent at it. But I was still nowhere near what I would have called healthy. After years of working to change this, however, I managed to reduce my weight and improve my health.

My main journey began in fourth grade when I started martial arts. I was young and had just moved to Wisconsin. My little brother was interested in joining martial arts, so I decided to tag along. I first decided to participate in the introductory classes and then decided to keep going.

I worked my way up through the belt ranks and eventually everything fell into place.

I earned my black belt, and then things really took off.

Appearing on ESPN, winning world championship titles, teaching classes, coaching the junior varsity team, and enjoying it all, I had created a better life for myself. I learned to put in the time and to strive for major goals. I discovered that exercise made me feel better, and I ate healthier.

All of that changed in the middle of my junior year of high school. I underwent invasive hip surgery that put my martial arts career on hold. The surgeon discovered a benign tumor in conjunction with the slew of other issues in my hip. My entire athletic career seemed like it had simply been launched off the tracks.

In the year leading up to this surgery, though, I could sense things weren't going well. I wasn't competing at the same level. I knew that my body couldn't take it, but I pushed through anyway. I wanted to win, and I did. But I reached a low point at the time of surgery. I had let my body suffer at the expense of my athletic achievements. That year I had appeared on ESPN, won my age division for the year, won in Quebec and in Dublin. In that same year, however, I had hobbled in pain and collapsed mid-competition. I had reached both ends of the extreme.

Through this experience, though, I discovered more about myself. I had fallen down, and I needed to get back up. It was the simple oscillating curve of life, but I had learned what I was capable of. My body had been beaten down throughout the competition year, and topped off with surgery, but now it was time to heal, time to get stronger.

Post-surgery pushed me to alter my overall perspective. Without being able to work out, I still worked to build my body into what I believed it could be. By eating even healthier, I managed to feel healthier even with the lack of exercise. While I surely had lost muscle during this recovery period, I had not completely wasted the time.

After numerous weeks on crutches, months of physical therapy, and a change of perspective, I was fully on the path to recovery. From there, I looked into what I could do to build myself back up. My dad had always been an active runner, so I decided to follow that path.

I slowly worked my way up to training for numerous hours a week once again. I set my ambitions high, as I looked to complete my first half marathon, then to finish my first full marathon. I trained with my dad throughout the entire process. Encouraging and motivating each other, we accomplished each mission.

Moving away from how I have personally managed my health, however, we can look at the bigger picture. Society works in a much different way. The current flaw in how people approach health revolves around a timetable. People want to live healthy lifestyles, but they want it immediately, a one-day, cure-all-my-issues type of success program—when in reality, this doesn't exist. People are thus met with quick, short-term diets that feel like they could work.

This methodology is all wrong, however. Health is forever ongoing. There is no one-stop cure for health. Instead, you must invest in and maintain your health throughout your life, otherwise it will deteriorate. Health is a major asset that continues to depreciate, but if taken care of, you can leverage it for your entire life.

And much like Ray Kroc's unwitting impact on the health of the United States at large, today's innovators are likely to offer a unique approach to addressing health through a wave of other innovations related to an increasingly individual-istic consumer:

We want it our way.

"The idea is, we want you to unlock different food based on your taste and nutrition," Sweetgreen Co-CEO Jonathan Neman told Forbes, describing a menu that, when viewed on the app, might look one way to a lactose-intolerant Harvest Bowl lover and a different way to a vegetarian Shroomami customer. "The Sweetgreen of the future is dynamic and based on preferences."[11]

And innovators like Neman and Sweetgreen are just the tip of the iceberg.

To understand the future of fast-food innovation and its innovators, I embarked on a yearlong quest to discover the future by:

- Speaking with influencers at established fast-food giants from McDonald's to Chipotle.
- Interviewing new innovators at upstart food ventures—some with a single location and others with their first dozen.
- Studying technology players supporting ordering, delivery, supply chain, location selection, marketing automation, and menu development.
- Engaging with bleeding edge consumers obsessed with nutrition and wellness, including Division I athletes at Ohio University, the Georgia Institute of Technology, and Drexel University.

---

11   Ibid

- Compiling my own research on various companies, trends, and government-issued recommendations to back this analysis.

As a result, I've identified five core trends poised to transform the way we quickly eat food in the future:

1. Health, as consumers search for options that align to a changing health-conscious consumer.
2. Diversity, as consumers look beyond the "burger and fries" fare to unique combinations such as ethnic dishes from new and exotic locations.
3. Safety, as consumers examine supply-chain safety, express concerns about bioterrorism, and want to understand options for tracking sourcing of raw ingredients.
4. Convenience, as consumers explore ways to get their food delivered, picked up, brought by food trucks, and centralized in new locations.
5. Social Conscience, as consumers look to ensure employees are paid well, environmental concerns are addressed, and values of the companies fit their aims.

* * *

Throughout this book, you'll see the intersection between these trends and quick-service restaurants—including fast-food and fast-casual dining locations. Those who believe the restaurant business is too risky to enter are missing the full story. Today, in an ever-changing culture, even our outlook on food has evolved. Instead of the old, out-of-date view on quick service restaurants, we have a much more advanced approach to food.

Food is evolving.

Slowly being integrated into our lives are nutritious meals from new, innovative restaurants. The towering dominance of major chains such as McDonald's is now being challenged by established competitors like Chipotle and newer entrants such as Sweetgreen. Beyond this development, the overall food environment has faced rapidly changing trends. No longer do a cheeseburger and fries qualify as a feel-good meal. Given this, it's time for the industry to change as well.

As time goes on, the overall food industry is sure to adapt to key consumer preferences. While food service is tough, there are new opportunities quickly gaining traction throughout the United States today.

* * *

It's my hope that this book will resonate with those inter-ested in learning about trends occurring throughout the fast-service dining industry in America. Current and future entrepreneurs of quick-service restaurants may specifically be interested as the book looks to capitalize on future opportunities. Outside of entrepreneurs, students looking to learn more about the food industry and companies looking to hear a new perspective regarding their industry may be interested in reading this book.

The underlying ideology here uses a forward-thinking approach regarding the QSR market, which allows for capitalization on projected future trends. Built upon this is the definition of health and how health in the United States is changing. Moreover, these ideas have been compiled to analyze the market and potentially lead new entrants into it.

Beyond that, I have thoughtfully projected the future operations of the QSR market. Given my research, new entrants to the healthy, QSR market should have an understanding of various trends currently being implemented, and how to initiate future action in order to derive success while competing in the market.

CHAPTER TWO

WHAT IS A QSR?

———

Created to include modern food trends in America's ever-changing culture, the term quick-service restaurant (QSR) was branded.

Q.S.R. — QSR Magazine explains what the implications of a QSR really include. This term encompasses fast-food restaurants and newer fast-casual restaurants. QSR Magazine defines a QSR as much more than a nicer line of fast-food restaurants, however.

Scott Davis, chief concept officer at Panera Bread, a prominent QSR, stated that "for [Panera], we look at the whole package. It's not just the food. It's not just the décor. ... It's a mindset."[12]Kevin Moll, CEO of National Restaurant Consultants Inc., sees QSRs as an opportunity to demonstrate a "brand's strengths in a compelling, value-oriented fashion to the consumer."[13]

Moll additionally discusses the actual implications of QSRs. "Today's restaurant operators are selling to a consumer who has been financially impacted in a negative way, and as such, this consumer is specifically looking for two things: convenience and value," described Moll, whose firm helps fast-food clients with their marketing initiatives. "If the marketing proposal misses these two targets, it will not be effective."[14]

As for a less professional view on QSRs, that still stands moderately true, Urban Dictionary describes a QSR as such:

> Abbreviation for Quick Service Restaurant, the modern [politically correct] way to say Fast Food Restaurant. Instead of being seated at a table, placing your order with the waitstaff, and the food is brought to you on dishes — QSR has a drive-thru or you place your order with a cashier at the front counter

---

12   "The New Definition of "Fast Food". *QSR Magazine*. April 19, 2010. Accessed April 07, 2019. https://www.qsrmagazine.com/news/new-definition-fast-food.

13   Ibid

14   Ibid

and take the food in a bag or similar disposable carrier. The food is mostly pre-packaged and reheated, so you get your food faster than if it were made to order. "Fast food" carries a negative connotation as unhealthy, so the industry uses QSR instead to avoid the stigma and to account for the increasingly high-priced "premium" fast food options.[15]

Whatever perception someone has of QSRs, however, many of the characteristics remain the same. A QSR encompasses change and innovation. Simple fast food was the past, and now it is time for a rebranding revolution where QSRs can take the stage.

In addition, building from Moll's statement, QSRs work to offer larger value to their consumers, often at the expense of higher prices to consumers. This stems from the reaction to America slowly noticing the issues present in society surrounding health and food initiatives. QSR innovations are a direct result of this, in an attempt to slim down the U.S. obesity epidemic.

* * *

---

15 "QSR." *Urban Dictionary.* Accessed April 07, 2019. https://www. urbandictionary.com/define.php?term=QSR.

Restaurants focused on speed have been around for a long time.

The evolution of fast food really took off after the creation of the Ford Model-T. According to a Modern Marvels documentary, *Drive-Thru*, this is where Americans were first given their very own sense of speed. While there were no fast-food drive-through locations for a substantial period after the presence of the first automobile, the new innovation quickly forced gas stations to evolve into the first generation of drive-throughs. While these locations did not serve food, they were serviced without the customer having to leave the comfort of their car.[16]

This all eventually changed, however. According to a report from the University of Michigan, "in 1921, two men—J.G. Kirby and Dr. Reuben W. Jackson—revolutionized the restaurant industry. They introduced the first drive-in restaurant known as the Texas Pig Stand—a barbeque-themed curbside service located off a busy highway in Dallas, Texas. Customers sat in their automobiles as 'tray boys delivered barbeque pork and Coca-Colas.'"[17]

---

16 "FAST FOOD: The Fast Lane of Life [MODERN MARVELS FULL DOCUMENTARY}." YouTube video, 44:02. "Documentaries Unlimited," February 26, 2014. https://youtu.be/BPf22nRVy2I.

17 Drive-in Restaurant. Accessed March 30, 2019. http://umich.edu/~drivein/restaurant.html.

Similar to everything else, however, the typical 'tray boys" standard evolved and was replaced. Fast food in this era experienced its own massive shift in trends as tray boys were often dropped and women were hired in their place. As Modern Marvels stated, "sex sells," and with this change, women had to wear revealing clothing to attract customers.[18] This approach was introduced to create a unique appeal over the competition in an already highly concentrated market. Fast-food owners went to all extremes to take customers away from the competition.

Then, another major change infiltrated the market. McDonald's was the first to cut its menu down to only a small selection of items and operate purely on speed. It cut out the tray boy operations and had customers walk up to its window to order, streamlining the process.

An era was forever changed from this point on. People interested in the food industry from all around visited the famed McDonald brothers' restaurant in hopes of finding out what made them so successful. Their speedy operations clearly stood as their competitive advantage over everyone else. After

---

18 "FAST FOOD: The Fast Lane of Life [MODERN MARVELS FULL DOCUMENTARY}." YouTube video, 44:02. "Documentaries Unlimited," February 26, 2014. https://youtu.be/BPf22nRVy2I.

ordering, McDonald's could provide customers their order in as little as fifteen seconds![19]

The playing field was forever changed. From here, many looked to duplicate this system. A lot of these companies still stand today, such as Taco Bell, Burger King, and Wendy's.

Fast food was launched from the ability to quickly go to-and-from places. From here, food companies followed the trend and sped up their own operations to keep pace.

* * *

Food trends today are changing once again.

Quick service restaurants are not solely focused on fifteen-second turnaround times or using car hops to serve customers anymore. Instead, they are looking at technology and societal impacts. QSRs are finally touching the boundaries of food classified as healthy. They're looking to differentiate themselves from one another, but this time it's through a strong mission and high standards.

Food is evolving, and we will take an in-depth look at what's happening now and where we're going in the future.

_____

19   Ibid

CHAPTER THREE

FOOD BEHEMOTHS

——

BIG BUSINESS IS BIG BUSINESS

Those categorized as giants in any industry stand upon insurmountable, constantly changing variables. As competition seems limited in the grand scheme of operation, society holds big businesses to a certain standard.

Businesses in today's era have a bad reputation. There's a negative connotation surrounding business operations, one owed to the profit-seeking executives, the "snaky" individuals studying business in school, and the corrupt actions of businesspeople worldwide. But a business is simply a tool to operate from.

A business is not inherently evil. Instead, it's a platform for value to be created and traded fairly. As we progress as a society, businesses should come to be used as tools for good.

Businesses can engage in social action in locations worldwide and, in doing so, promote the well-being of all people. Through a commitment to certain key initiatives, business can build a better society.

While businesses have the opportunity to create major change in the world (ideally for the better), they often fall short on their social missions. Companies are often stretched thin by pressure from investors to deliver increasing value year after year. Companies worry that participating in social initiatives will cut into corporate profits.

Numerous examples illustrate this dynamic. We can start by looking at the increase in obesity as fast-food restaurants have become more prevalent in the United States. Fast food is not the single determining factor in the U.S. obesity epidemic, yet fast-food restaurants have taken the heat for this issue.

Food is a major factor in everyone's life. The physiological need to eat and drink plays a crucial role in how humans operate day to day, thus this industry is capable of driving influential changes in how people live their lives. As of now, however, well-known players in the industry have not fully attacked the obesity epidemic. Instead, they have preserved their revenue, which leaves a gap in the market for new establishments.

Healthier QSRs are on the up and up. For restaurants offering a healthy menu, there may be a bigger picture than the simple salad being served. Restaurants have the opportunity to innovate their operations to account for the well-being of individuals. While fast food has taken the blame for the obesity epidemic, maybe it's possible to counteract this reputation.

In the United States, obesity affects nearly 40 percent of all adults[20] —but being overweight is not just a numbers issue. Food is a trickle-down influencer. Health care is an industry currently influenced by food, but in the future, transportation, architecture, and countless other industries may be altered due to our (literally) huge problem.

Companies have begun to take on these large societal issues. New ideology has taken over as corporate action takes the form of environmentally friendly initiatives, sustainable operations, and morally correct procedures inside and outside companies.

---

20 "Adult Obesity Facts | Overweight & Obesity | CDC." *Centers for Disease Control and Prevention.* Accessed April 07, 2019. https:// www.cdc.gov/obesity/data/adult.html.

This attempt to bring good into the world defines the new age of corporate operations. Nearly all major businesses have worked to embrace some form of corporate social responsibility (CSR) in order to better our society.

Big business has long embodied the act of squishing the little guy to solely increase corporate profit: this is the idea of the shareholder model. Yet businesses should not only focus on those who have invested in them and own them on the public market. For companies, many core values can be diminished as the investor's best interests overcome the company's real objective. This objective could theoretically provide satisfaction for the consumer, but that is often not the case. While this theme may occur anywhere, a shareholder perspective seems to present it more often. Instead, businesses should use a stakeholder model and work to account for all factors present in their industry.

Capitalizing on a stakeholder model can reinforce a brand reputation. For any startup QSR, a good reputation can be the determining factor in survival and long-term growth. Beyond that, using a stakeholder model can promote the satisfaction of employees, suppliers, and manufacturers, with investors also playing a role in this corporate strategy.

By using a stakeholder model, as opposed to a strictly shareholder model, businesses can climb the social ladder faster than competitors. By working to improve the overall experience everyone has interacting with the corporation, companies can easily elevate the perceived quality of the brand.

That being said, however, businesses must continue to operate. Trying to account for all potential events in the market would require an unfathomable number of resources, and for a company to work at all, money must be coming in, and people must be buying products. This is the simple structure for continued operations in the future.

From here, the big question stands: how can a company actually help the world?

For any major organization, the answer to that question will be echoed down from the top. A firm's leadership serves as the heart and soul of the company. While more simply put as the president or CEO, the leadership within a company can carry major influence at any point throughout the corporate hierarchy.

Looking at leadership throughout the fast-food industry, we can see a legend to the game in McDonald's franchisor Ray Kroc. This man worked diligently his entire life to become successful. He always had new sales gimmicks and worked hard to earn a respectable living—and he eventually became the man to grow a small restaurant into the largest one on the planet.

While Kroc entwined the growth strategy in the soul of McDonald's, innovation had always run through the veins of the burger operation—originally owned by the McDonald brothers. The brand ran successfully because of numerous key actions the brothers had implemented: they found success, for example, through heat lamps to ensure warm food, which allowed for the company to streamline operations. Additionally, certain technological factors allowed them to increase production. With such techniques, McDonald's had always been an innovative restaurant.

Kroc looked at McDonald's through a certain lens. As he said about the burger franchise, "We provide food that customers love, day after day after day. People just want more of it."[21] The corporation has been focused on providing value to the customer, a notion deeply rooted in the daily operations since Kroc stepped in as the ultimate franchisor of McDonald's.

Kroc's passion led to—and promoted—value creation operations for McDonald's. Even after his death, Kroc's version of McDonald's still works to provide the most customer-centered experience of all time.

---

21   "Ray Kroc Quotes." *BrainyQuote*. Accessed May 29, 2019. https://www.brainyquote.com/quotes/ray_kroc_173417.

He didn't have an easy journey. As Kroc noted on the McDonald's corporate website, "I was an overnight success alright, but 30 years is a long, long night."[22] Like many other visionaries, he put in immense work before his eventual streak of success. His success in scaling the McDonald's brand from a single restaurant in California to the largest restaurant chain in the world derived from his constant drive for achievement.

Additionally, Kroc had an alternative philosophy that set him apart from the field of competition. According to the McDonald's website:

> Ray Kroc wanted to build a restaurant system that would be famous for providing food of consistently high quality and uniform methods of preparation. He wanted to serve burgers, fries and beverages that tasted just the same in Alaska as they did in Alabama. To achieve this, he chose a unique path: persuading both franchisees and suppliers to buy into his vision, working not for McDonald's but for themselves, together with McDonald's. He promoted the slogan,

---

22 "Our History: Ray Kroc & The McDonald's Brothers | McDonald's." Our History: Ray Kroc & The McDonald's Brothers | McDonald's. Accessed April 07, 2019. https://www.mcdonalds.com/us/en-us/about-us/our-history.html.

"In business for yourself, but not by yourself."
His philosophy was based on the simple principle of a 3-legged stool: one leg was McDonald's franchisees; the second, McDonald's
suppliers; and the third, McDonald's employees. The stool was only as strong as the three
legs that formed its foundation.[23]

Kroc rocked the restaurant industry by reinventing the standard to which each individual store location was held.

With this three-legged stool vision, McDonald's crafted an
ideology that has allowed for strong brand cohesion. Franchisees, suppliers, and employees can clearly see their importance in the corporation.

While the franchisee model is not applicable to all quick-service restaurants, this model still applies. Instead of franchisees, QSRs can look to their corporate-owned stores instead.
Beyond this, though, suppliers and employees are an integral
part of business operations. Moreover, these three legs all
help provide the customer with the best experience possible. The customer is the most important aspect of running
a business, and McDonald's focuses on this principle in all
aspects of its operations.

---

23 Ibid

Customers: the driving force behind all business operations. How do you incentivize them, how do you build their trust, and how do you find a way to earn a profit? These questions are all considered while trying to please the targeted demographic.

THE POWER OF SCALE

With its brand name, a character named Ronald, and the recognizable golden arches, only one brand can come to mind. McDonald's.

McDonald's has created a brand that can be seen everywhere. You can travel through nearly every city in the United States and experience the vast array of fast-food restaurants, all lined up next to one another. While this is engrained in standard American culture, McDonald's stretches beyond the standard. The mega-restaurant has been able to scale its core operations to such a large degree that it can completely shift the marketplace.

One particular example of this is McDonald's use of blueberries.

Picture McDonald's fresh yogurt blueberry parfait. I bet you didn't know it even had this on the menu.

The current formulation of this blueberry parfait uses frozen blueberries; if McDonald's decided to alter its recipe to include fresh blueberries instead, grocery stores throughout the country would be blueberryless.

The true size of McDonald's became evident I interviewed a manager at McDonald's. To protect the identity of this manager, I will refer to her as Megan Anderson. While interviewing Anderson, she thoughtfully emphasized the pure scale that McDonald's operates with worldwide.

With McDonald's having such a wide influence in the world, it is no surprise that the chain has such a strong grip on the food industry. By simply changing one ingredient—even in a less popular item, such as the blueberry parfait—the entire dynamic of food operations could change nationwide.

* * *

To build a company, the customer must always come first. The mega-restaurant has focused on this customer-centric approach in to stay ahead of the game. By pleasing customers and listening to what they really want, not just what they say they want, McDonald's has been able to capitalize on this.

When you look at the numbers, money matters. Even when the market seems to be shifting toward healthy alternatives,

McDonald's customers are not looking to spend excessive amounts on salads and veggie burgers, and McDonald's knows that.

However, as McDonald's continues to emphasize its customer-centric ideology, it has implemented new strategies to complete customers' requests. Cage-free eggs, for example, have been a key element in turning McDonald's into a more ethical and socially responsible corporation.

However, due to the scale of McDonald's, even attempting this change was not possible back in 2018. There were not enough cage-free chicken farms in existence for McDonald's to successfully source from—not to mention the domino effect that occurred after McDonald's made the switch. Since then, many other companies have also made the transition to ethical sourcing operations.

> At McDonald's, we're making changes based on what we're hearing from all of you. That's why we work hard to make tasty food with a "less is more" philosophy. But what does that mean for our ingredients? … To put it frankly, it means — The Simpler The Better™.[24]

---

24 Ibid

This statement demonstrates McDonald's commitment to its customers in the form of listening to what they prefer and working to ease their worries. The overall dedication to customers is shown throughout the various strategy initiatives that McDonald's has pledged to implement.

"We are customer fanatics at McDonald's," Anderson said.

This constant focus on providing value to customers is the exact philosophy that has been deeply rooted in McDonald's ideology since the beginning. Furthermore, this idea of pleasing the customer has been a major factor in keeping the doors open and the lights on.

By revolving operations around strong core values, McDonald's has been able to continuously stay on top, even with vast competition in the fast-food market. The continuous adaptation to consumer demands illustrates this commitment.

All-day breakfast exemplifies this commitment to customers. With other fast-food restaurants running all-day breakfast options, McDonald's needed to please consumers with a release of its own initiative. Going further, the chain worked to add its favored items onto the breakfast menu all day to please the customer at all hours of operation.

Since the initial franchising of McDonald's, Ray Kroc's influence has continued to stick with the company. Based on the firm's current operations, the ideology from its founder is still held dear. The commitment to customer satisfaction, a commitment to quality and speed, and a commitment to doing what you love are all shown in the strategy rolled out from corporate McDonald's.

While McDonald's has shown continued attentiveness to its customers from day one, other companies have approached their operations in a slightly different manner. The extreme speed of a standard fast-food restaurant has not been carried throughout all operations in the current era of modern dining. While evolving dining methods continue to grow, fast-casual dining has allowed new companies to enter the market. Well-known, well-established fast-casual restaurants have infiltrated the diets of millions of Americans.

REVOLUTIONIZE, INNOVATE, & COMPETE

We are Panera Bread. And we believe that good food, food you can feel good about, can bring out the best in all of us. Food served in a warm, welcoming environment, by people

who care. To us, that's good eating and that's
why we're here.[25]

The decadent taste of hot mac and cheese, a fancy presentation in the depths of a bread bowl, the cold, crisp flavor of a unique beverage—Panera Bread has it all.

Panera is a QSR that has tapped into a slightly healthier market than stereotypical fast-food restaurants and is now a part of JAB Holding Company. While it has not technically branded as a pure health company, the firm looks to exhibit healthier options in its salads and sandwiches. Often still loaded with calories and carbohydrates, the latter half of Panera's brand name is often served with meals: bread.

Panera has still lacked the full composition of a fully health-conscious brand. With a bakery selling many less-than-nutritional items, and a drink menu full of sugar, Panera has work to do before representing the ideal diet. Yet, given its health-focused menu in comparison to competitors, Panera has been able to compete as the health-conscious competitor in the marketplace.

Panera Bread has been a national leader in the food industry. Back in 2010, Panera was the first restaurant in the country

25 "We Are Panera Bread." *Panera Bread.* Accessed April 7, 2019.
    https://www.panerabread.com/en-us/company/about-panera.html.

whose menu boards gave calorie information. The company has taken action to be transparent on what is going into its food and what consumers are putting into their bodies. This dedication to improving certain health aspects has continuously been shown in daily operations. Panera's commitment in June 2014 to rid its food of "artificial colors, sweeteners, flavors, and preservatives" shows how the company has continued to evolve; this goal was eventually reached in January 2017.[26]

Panera's actions have surely made an impact. With its relatively clean menu, customers are pushed to feel as though they are receiving a healthy meal. I have personally been appreciative of this mission.

Omaha, Nebraska, has tons of food, and I, along with most everyone else, really, ~really~ enjoy it. However, not many restaurants have any sort of appeal to a healthy lifestyle. Trying to balance a job, school, extracurriculars, a social life, and whatever else can push people to the limit for time. For me, Panera is a quick, healthier option than the typical fast-food joint.

And Panera understands what we, the consumers, want out of a quick meal. Panera Bread Company CEO Ron Shaich

---

26 "We Are Panera Bread." *Panera Bread.* Accessed April 7, 2019. https://www.panerabread.com/en-us/company/about-panera.html.

emphasized that "our complete focus is on where the world is going."[27] The company has continued to evolve within the marketplace to stay competitive. With health trends sweeping the United States, Panera aims to capitalize on this trend.

With seven in ten adults attempting to eat healthier at restaurants than what they ate two years ago, consumers are shifting towards a health-conscious perspective on the dining experience.[28] Panera Bread has been able to target this market – presumably our market – with their specialized menu for the health-conscious consumer. With entrees including more natural ingredients than competitors, while keeping the nutrients in check, Panera is able to entice their target market.

Another way that the company is working to push and follow trends is their advancement of ethical food operations. Panera's 2014 ethical initiative of reducing confinement of pigs, and the 2015 initiative to shift towards cage free eggs, shows the company's ability to operate at a higher standard.[29]

27 Meyer, Zlati, and Charisse Jones. "How Panera Won the Restaurant Game." *USA Today*. April 06, 2017. Accessed April 07, 2019. https://www.usatoday.com/story/money/business/2017/04/06/how-panera-won-restaurant-game/100072546/.

28 "Public Views About Americans' Eating Habits." *Pew Research Center Science & Society*. December 1, 2016. Accessed June 14, 2019. https://www.pewresearch.org/science/2016/12/01/public-views-about-americans-eating-habits/.

29 "We Are Panera Bread." *Panera Bread*. Accessed April 7, 2019. https://www.panerabread.com/en-us/company/about-panera.html.

These ethical implications have evolved in America over time. From Upton Sinclair's *The Jungle* to modern food concerns, there has always been ethical and social concerns related to how the entirety of the food process is controlled.

No longer are we living in a world where mystery processes can occur. Transparency on the back end has been long desired, and the consumers are finally starting to see this come to fruition.

The ethical implications of human nutrition have been a point of concern. Looking at industry leaders, therefore, we see the changing patterns in how companies operate. More than likely, these companies will also upgrade to industry standards quickly before losing out on lost revenue by seeming outdated. When one company makes a major change, many will follow.

While both Panera and McDonald's operate with extreme success, they promote their influence through certain key operational efficiencies. Drivers, if you will, of success can be shown through a tactical approach that often reduces costs and bumps up bottom-line earnings. From these key drivers, the major players—or food behemoths—are able to capture their portion of the market.

INNOVATING CORPORATE SUCCESS

"No lettuce, tomatoes, mayo, or onions please," I would ask my mom to say whenever I ordered a cheeseburger while going through the drive-through line as a kid. It felt like every time, however, they would get something wrong. As a picky eater, I found eating at fast-food restaurants somewhat difficult growing up. There was always a mistake in my meal, or someone else's. And not only small mistakes—issues here ranged from inaccurate meals to entire entrees missing.

"How can a restaurant mess up so bad?" my family often questioned.

While these errors seemed to occur regularly when I was a child, service has seemingly improved. After all the mistakes fast food restaurants have made over the years, endless innovations have arisen to address them—especially as of lately. Restaurants have been able to advance operations to please the consumer even more. While orders may still contain mistakes, overall quality for most brands seems to be continuously improving, in part because of the technological advancements occurring within the brick-and-mortar storefront.

Returning to restaurant superpowers, I first learned about the operational successes of fast-food restaurants through a research project in high school. By being able to change how typical restaurant operations occur, companies have managed to simplify their entire in-store process. To paraphrase what was done to drive success: massive corporations can limit the impact of human error on their operations.

I'm not saying robots are working behind the counter, but there are certainly mechanisms in place to help team members. I have personally seen the limited culinary skills required to operate many kitchens. While sit-down restaurants operate far beyond this scope and require years of experience to manage, fast-food restaurants have simply taken the greatest difficulties out of the kitchen. Where a professional chef must manage flavors and a variety of other factors, quick-service restaurants have their cooking down to a precise science. Engineering feats behind restaurant equipment appear to be a major driver behind QSR success.

While food employees are given rapid orders, their skills lie apart from those of culinary professionals. Instead, employees work through the smaller details at rapid paces to please both the drive-through line and the crowd up front. While good employees are a vital component of QSR operations, many companies have taken the majority of human risk out of operating.

Technological advancements have continued to alter the way restaurants operate. From these advancements, human error has been continually diminished. While issues can still arise, companies have streamlined the process to achieve success.

* * *

From simply walking into a newer restaurant, you can tell aspects of operation have changed since their founding. Observe the next time you enter a restaurant. After the first few steps inside the restaurant, you'll see television screens covering the wall behind the checkout counter. These categorized screens show different deals, meals, and all sorts of menu options. You'll see a kitchen full of high-tech kitchen appliances, an updated interface nearby, a specialized payment software to allow for ease of operation, and so on. Firms have worked to simplify use for both customers and employees.

The appeal of this technology-infused lifestyle has been a long time in the making. From this, many restaurants have worked to add easy-to-use technology into their store locations. With television screens displaying the menu and innovative payment systems at the checkout counter, restaurants have implemented more than just these newer features.

Looking at other changes with the front-end efforts of fast food restaurants, shiny Coca-Cola machines stand with a wide selection of drinks. Many brands, many flavors, carbonated, and uncarbonated—these state-of-the-art machines have expanded the choices consumers have. Technological advancements have changed the way we go about drinking soft drinks.

Kids growing up in this technologically advanced era won't just experience the mixture of ten or so different sodas all combined; they'll have the opportunity to mix hundreds of soda flavors together in any sort of wacky concoction they choose.

Moving forward, from just a snapshot look at technology involved in a physical store, there have been changes rapidly occurring to restaurant operations as technology continues to evolve. The advancements made here allow companies to streamline their operating costs, as companies can work to maximize their bottom-line earnings. While profit isn't the only factor driving these changes, companies are working to improve aspects of their restaurant to give the customer the best experience possible.

With the advancements of certain aspects within the food industry, restaurants nationwide are continually upgrading their operations. This continued need to innovate drives corporate success for these major food firms, operating both nationally and abroad. From various key productivity drivers, major food corporations are able to effectively influence the food industry in countless manners.

CHAPTER FOUR

WHAT IT MEANS
TO BE HEALTHY

———

The night began as a typical Friday night for many college students. Ben Widmann, a Division I collegiate wrestler for Ohio University, had been enjoying a good meal with friends: a juicy cheeseburger on a thick bun with crispy and salty French fries, a classic staple meal for an enjoyable Friday night.

"Mm, this cheeseburger is so good," he told his friends passionately.

It wasn't often that he enjoyed an unhealthy meal in the fall, especially with wrestling season right around the corner. "I might have to go back up for another," he exclaimed, standing

WHAT IT MEANS TO BE HEALTHY · 53

up to search out a second dinner. Widmann told himself he had eaten healthy all week anyway. He was prepared to eat a hefty meal.

As the wrestling season was not yet in full swing, the stringent diet of a Division I athlete was not yet being strictly enforced. Even though Widmann had a morning workout the next day—weight training—the thought that his meal the day before would affect his performance the next day had not crossed his mind. He had been healthy all week long. He deserved to eat one good-tasting meal without having to think about what he was putting into his body, right?

Maybe.

* * *

According to the American College of Sports Medicine, "Adequate food and fluid should be consumed before, during, and after exercise to help maintain blood glucose concentration during exercise, maximize exercise performance, and improve recovery time. Athletes should be well hydrated before exercise and drink enough fluid during and after exercise to balance fluid losses."[30] This is great and all, but it doesn't really mean anything.

---

30 "Food as Fuel Before, During and After Workouts." *American Heart Association*. January 2, 2015. https://www.heart.org/en/

You should obviously eat healthy and stay hydrated, but how does that actually work?

Eva Selhub, M.D., a writer for Harvard Health Publishing, explained the role food plays as fuel for the brain: "like an expensive car, your brain functions best when it gets only premium fuel. Eating high-quality foods that contain lots of vitamins, minerals, and antioxidants nourishes the brain and protects it from oxidative stress — the 'waste' (free radicals) produced when the body uses oxygen, which can damage cells."[31]

"Unfortunately, just like an expensive car, your brain can be damaged if you ingest anything other than premium fuel," Dr. Selhub wrote. "If substances from 'low-premium' fuel (such as what you get from processed or refined foods) get to the brain, it has little ability to get rid of them. Diets high in refined sugars, for example, are harmful to the brain. In addition to worsening your body's regulation of insulin, they also promote inflammation and oxidative stress."[32]

healthy-living/healthy-eating/eat-smart/nutrition-basics/food-as-fuel-before-during-and-after-workouts.

31   Selhub, Eva. 2018. "Nutritional Psychiatry: Your Brain on Food." *Harvard Health Blog.* April 5, 2018. https://www.health.harvard.edu/blog/nutritional-psychiatry-your-brain-on-food-201511168626.

32   Ibid

While this specifically looks at the brain, the complexity of the human body means these issues of mind and body are intertwined. The impact that food has on your brain therefore has a major impact on the rest of your body.

As Dr. Selhub illustrated, what you eat can really have an effect on how you live your life. The various chemical compounds released within your body can alter the everyday fabric of daily life.

Simply put, food matters.

* * *

For wrestler Ben Widmann, the next morning came extremely quick.

He was laying in his dorm room, with the sun shining brightly on his bed, and he slowly woke up. Thinking nothing of the delicious meal the night before, he got out of bed to get ready for the day. He prepared himself for his team's morning workout.

Even without thinking about the night before, Widmann still moved quite sluggishly in the morning. Given Widmann's typical college student sleep schedule, he found morning practices particularly ruthless. Nonetheless, he made his way to the gym not too far from his dormitory.

The food from the night before, while unnoticed, was still sitting heavy in his stomach. He was not prepared for what the coach had in store. Widmann worked to achieve results during his workout, only to fall short each time as he lacked the necessary strength.

"AGHHHHH," he grunted at the gym as he lifted weights. He could feel he wasn't up to his full potential. He was lifting a normal weight but couldn't finish each set.

"Ben! Where is the rest of that set?" his coach yelled across the weight room at him.

Widmann, slightly disappointed, struggled through the rest of the workout that Saturday morning, his muscles barely able to produce enough output to move what he was lifting. With each set, he became more and more unengaged. As his muscles deteriorated, he found himself unable to perform at his best.

The meal from the previous night had been weighing him down.

He wasn't entirely sure why:

- Maybe it was the food itself—greasy, heavy, and loaded with the bad fats.
- Maybe it was the portions—too much food in too short a time.
- Maybe one of the ingredients was contaminated—perhaps he'd had a mild bout of food poisoning, not enough to be truly noticeable but enough to hurt his performance materially.
- Maybe it was the time—he'd eaten late, gone out to get it, and affected his sleep schedule rather than opting for delivery.

The main thing to recognize is that food—not only *what* he ate, but also when, why, where, and how—all affected key aspects of his performance. And all of us, whether we are extreme athletes or not, are impacted by our food too.

For a high-performing athlete, the cheeseburger, fries, and entire second dinner after that halted Widmann's progress in the weight room. He couldn't channel enough strength to successfully grow as an athlete, an unwanted result especially throughout the preseason.

He was letting himself down.

The next day, however, he changed.

He didn't want to appear weak in the weight room when he knew he had more. Driven to impress the coaches as well, he decided to change his approach to practice. He was ready for the next workout. In preparation, he went to a healthy dining hall closer to the athlete dorms on Ohio's campus.

He fueled himself with healthy greens, lean meats, and good carbs. His first plate overflowed with vegetables, mimicking a rainbow, and his second plate featured a simple grilled chicken breast with some whole grains—in sum, Widmann ate much healthier this time around. The goal was to shape himself into a competitive wrestler on the Division I stage. To do so, he knew he would need to excel in the weight room, on the mats, and in the kitchen—or, in his case, Ohio University's dining halls. This certainly showed the next morning while at his morning lift.

While food may go in without many consequences, what your body produces may be completely different. Unhealthy eating leads to an unhealthy lifestyle, but by eating healthy meals, there are external benefits beyond simply nutrition.

Food has the capacity to affect everyday life, and we can harness that in one particular way: willpower. By staying conscientious about what we eat, we can control how food impacts our everyday life. Eat healthy, and live a healthy lifestyle. Eat poorly, and the negative effects of food are sure to follow. By changing the way that we eat, we can build ourselves into an entirely new character.

It goes beyond simply what we eat—and these trends are changing the way fast-food innovators look at their target consumer.

THE 'AVERAGE' AMERICAN

> *The Dietary Guidelines' Key Recommendations for healthy eating patterns should be applied in their entirety, given the interconnected relationship that each dietary component can have with others.*[33]

The wholistic approach to health points to the inner workings of the complex human body. With such a complicated way to define health, and actually *be* healthy, experts have taken it upon themselves to build a roadmap toward health.

By applying the Dietary Guidelines in their entirety, people would ideally walk away with a clear picture of how to eat, exercise, and live various other aspects of life in a healthy manner.

---

33 "Dietary Guidelines." *Office of Disease Prevention and Health Promotion.* March 11, 2019. Accessed April 07, 2019. https://health.gov/dietaryguidelines/.

The federal government releases updated versions of *The Dietary Guidelines* every five years. In the 2015–2020 updated version, there are many recommendations for how Americans should live their lives. In order to be healthy on average, there are certain steps individuals should take to minimize risk and maximize quality of life. Below is a mini breakdown of what the guidelines recommend with regard to regular eating patterns.

A healthy eating pattern includes:[34]

- A variety of vegetables from all the subgroups—dark green, red and orange, legumes (beans and peas), starchy, and other.
- Fruits, especially whole fruits.
- Grains, at least half of which are whole grains.
- Fat-free or low-fat dairy, including milk, yogurt, cheese, and/or fortified soy beverages.
- A variety of protein foods, including seafood, lean meats and poultry, eggs, legumes (beans and peas), and nuts, seeds, and soy products.
- Oils.

---

34   Ibid

A healthy eating pattern limits:[35]

- Saturated fats and *trans* fats.
- Added sugars.
- Sodium.

Beyond these recommendations, there is certainly greater depth. The average person should consume a mix of each food category regularly. Recommendations include 2.5 cups of vegetables per day, 2 cups of fruit per day, 6 ounces of grains per day, 3 cups of dairy per day, 5.5 ounces of protein foods per day, 27 grams of oils per day, and a limit of 270 calories for other foods that fall beyond the scope of these food groups.[36]

By eating a mix of food that pulls from various subgroups within each food category, individuals will be able to obtain greater amounts of nutrients needed to build the body. While many often fall into a habit of eating certain foods, branching out will allow the body to strengthen certain functions.

Food stands as the basis for health. No matter what goes into your body, if you take in less calories than your body burns throughout the day, you will lose weight. This is true even if you eat Doritos and Twinkies all day.

---

35 Ibid
36 Ibid

The same is true for gaining weight. If your caloric intake is greater than what your body uses throughout the day, you will begin to put on weight—even if you eat only healthy food all day. Thus food has the ability to impact numerous factors of daily life.

According to health.gov, "*Strong evidence shows that healthy eating patterns are associated with a reduced risk of cardiovascular disease* (CVD). *Moderate evidence indicates that healthy eating patterns also are associated with a reduced risk of type 2 diabetes, certain types of cancers* (such as colorectal and postmenopausal breast cancers), *overweight, and obesity. Emerging evidence also suggests that relationships may exist between eating patterns and some neurocognitive disorders and congenital anomalies.*"[37]

In the simplest terms, what you put into your body really does matter.

ACCESSING BEAST MODE

Rolling over the bright green grass on the gold and white car, Hannah Donahue stood tall and proud as she cheered for her favorite team. The roar of the crowd, the rumble of the car on the field—Hannah had been living the dream.

---

37   Ibid

"Go Georgia Tech!" she and her teammates yelled as they waved to the crowd.

Hannah had been cheering for only a short while with her new team at the time of this heated football game. She had already committed, however, to numerous workouts a week and living a healthy lifestyle to perform at her optimal level.

To be a Division I athlete, such as a cheerleader at Georgia Institute of Technology, you must undergo difficult situations to remain healthy. Beyond simple health, athletes work to build themselves into machines capable of specialized skills specific for their sports and events. For cheerleading, building muscle is huge.

Weight-lifting, cardio, diet: all broad aspects that must be carefully watched while working to perform. Looking specifically at Hannah's journey, she had always been physically fit enough for her desired activities, yet she had never focused on building muscle to better perform.

The image of health has altered the way athletes operate. To be healthy can mean numerous things. For real results, though, health should be defined as the point at which the probability of disease and medical complication is limited. So what does this actually look like? How can we see this? And how can we get to this point?

Hannah does numerous exercises to remain fit.

As she described, "I need to work out pretty often each week for cheerleading. On Tuesdays and Thursdays from 6 a.m. to 7:15 a.m., I have morning lift. Then, later in the day from 6 p.m. 'til 8:30 p.m. on Tuesdays and Thursdays, we have cheerleading practice. We also have tumbling practice and cardio each week."

This intense workout schedule, on top of taking a full course load as a computer science major at an elite university, can be pretty difficult. Time management can be challenging for many college students, especially when balancing difficult coursework with athletics.

While health encompasses more than exercise and nutrition, I will narrow in on these factors specifically. This book will continue to look more at physical health as opposed to a broader more inclusive term of health. Mental health, and a variety of other aspects of health, however, should certainly be incorporated into an overall understanding of a person's health.

Examining Hannah's nutrition, protein drinks are always provided and encouraged after a difficult weight-lifting session. To promote healthy muscle growth, healthy supplements are given to the Georgia Tech athletes. Hannah talked about how she enjoyed certain flavors of the protein drinks.

"I think they come in 26 grams and 42 grams of protein. I like the vanilla 42-gram protein drink or the 26-gram strawberry banana drink," she said with excitement.

Hannah also discussed the athlete-specific nutrition store where all athletes at Georgia Tech can go. She said how this allowed her to continue to eat healthy while on the go. This special store seems to have allowed her to stay fit while accommodating her busy schedule as a college student.

"They let us go in everyday and take just a few items. I usually go get a small carton of milk and a sandwich or a cheese stick or something after a working out," she explained. This allows her to take the complication out of considering what it means to stay healthy.

From a competitive cheerleader to a Division I collegiate cheerleader, Hannah has clearly made her progression up the competitive ladder. She overcame a back injury and now makes frequent appearances at Georgia Tech's sporting events. In making this jump to an even more competitive level, she now holds herself to a higher standard of healthiness.

As a Division I cheerleader, she must live up to certain expectations. Obviously, she is required to attend workouts and practices in order to show up at competitions and make appearances at different Georgia Tech sporting events. But the health qualifications for athletes in many sports go further than just this. Cheerleaders are not merely expected to *be* healthy; they must also *look* it.

This notion of a physically fit image poses another question on what it means to be healthy. Fitness means something different to every athlete. If we wanted to quantify it, we could potentially look at people's body mass index (BMI). But when a football player has obscenely larger muscles than an average person, they may be categorized as obese by this scale when in fact they are in phenomenal shape. Physical health is extremely difficult to quantify.

CRIPPLING AMERICAN OBESITY

The very unhealthy side of the health spectrum is all around us. Each day, people grapple with health complications because of obesity. Simply carrying the extra pounds has proven detrimental to our well-being as humans. The crippling American obesity that we live has simply gotten worse over the past few decades. Obesity rates have risen, and so has the pressure to stepping on the scale. But where is the pressure to change this?

Obesity rates in the United States are the highest they've ever been. Simply from the link to disease and an overall decrease in quality of life, obesity has drastically impacted individuals throughout the nation.

Moreover, obesity is not something that can be waved away with a vaccination or special prescription. There is not a quick fix for going from obesity to physical fitness—no matter how much we want to believe there is. Shifting from one end of the spectrum to the other takes time. As a result, difficulties lie ahead for the current status of American obesity. Weights are increasing, and issues continue to arise. But this current epidemic does not need to be our future.

* * *

Continuing on the topic of defining pure health, what does it really look like? The standard person would assume Division-I NCAA athletes are classified as healthy, but how healthy are they? Health seems to have a multidimensional spectrum attached to its classification. While individuals may be healthy in one sense, they may not be as healthy in another. However, looking at health simply, we can see clear divisions from very unhealthy to average to very healthy.

EXTREME ATHLETICISM

A 3x state champion and now a NCAA Division I athlete, Nick Manning (whose name has been changed for anonymity) competes for his university's wrestling team. Wearing his school's colors proudly, Manning works fiercely to stay competitive at his weight class. In order to compete with some of the best in the nation, Manning must constantly work to improve his physical abilities on the mats. Beyond this, he works diligently to stay healthy outside the training facilities as well. For Manning, nutrition is a major factor in his ability to wrestle.

Being healthy has always consisted of a much blander approach than many for him. He's never used a special fad diet or fat-burning technique. Instead, Manning approaches health through a strictly self-regulated diet followed by a number of workouts each week.

Four years, only. Five if an athlete redshirt. Either way, only a few years to perform as an NCAA athlete. Therefore, peak performance is a must during this duration to extract the greatest awards sports can offer. Competition at this level is high. However, athleticism can mean so many things for these athletes. In the case of Manning's commitment to wrestling, he has had extreme dedication to competing at the highest level.

During the summer offseason, Manning used his time in an extremely productive manner. He explained how he "was up early every day this past summer for 6 a.m. lifts. [Manning] needed to have a routine that allowed [him] to stay fit for wrestling while continuing to work a full-time job." His elite workout routine allowed him to structure various areas of his life. Even after work, he would go to the training facility to wrestle. He had to manage a schedule that would fit all of his workouts in each day, and that is exactly what he did. From his productive workout schedule, this action has trickled down to all aspects of his life.

Working hard has always helped Nick Manning build a healthy lifestyle for himself. He, however, takes his athleticism to the extreme. Beyond the workouts, Manning is very restrictive about what he eats in order to stay in shape for wrestling. While his routine falls on the extreme side of the health spectrum, it is a daily choice that he makes to stay healthy.

When asking about the nutritional restrictions he sticks to, Manning clearly illustrated his dedication. "I haven't had dessert since my freshman year of high school," he stated proudly. His initial calorie-cutting trick back in high school has now turned into a lifestyle for him. Skipping the after-dinner sweets has allowed him to meet his weight requirements for each wrestling meet.

"I also try to eat light during the wrestling season. I usually have a Clif Bar before my morning workout followed by Greek yogurt, chocolate milk, peanut butter crackers, raisins, and an apple. For lunch, I usually make a nice egg sandwich on a bagel. Then, I always make sure to eat a Clif Bar before my second workout of the day. After all this, though, I will usually have chicken, rice, and some Greek yogurt for dinner."

"[My wrestling team] will also undergo a dry season where nobody is supposed to drink alcohol," he explained. These procedures allow Manning to maintain a consistent weight, so he is ready for weigh-ins at each tournament he attends. The bland diet of chicken and rice also permits Manning to get his macronutrients without the additional calories. As for the dry season, wrestlers are held to a standard of staying clear of alcohol. With excessive calories in essentially every alcoholic drink, avoiding these more hidden calories allows wrestlers to maintain their weight by staying in caloric intake balance.

By looking at these stringent expectations that Manning experiences from himself and his coaches, it is clear that what it means to be healthy is different for him than the average American. Where a Division I athlete competes on an elite level, the average person simply doesn't need to operate at this capacity.

* * *

For a general American, there are guidelines for health. This outline of guidelines includes the most important aspects of general health.

And while these stories of extreme athletes who obsess over nutrition, exercise, and wellness may seem far removed from "average" Americans, we can rightly see these trends related to nutrition, health, food diversity, food safety, convenience, and social consciousness.

CHAPTER FIVE

HEALTH

———

Watch your cholesterol.

Make sure you don't eat too much sodium.

Stay away from processed foods.

Fat isn't healthy—but neither is low-fat.

Carbs are the enemy!

ALL FOOD IS BAD!

I don't have a degree in nutritional studies, but I have seen the claims, the recommendations from "expert" advocates, and the general lack of logic and consistency behind a majority of the hype.

Random, ridiculous claims have been made about what we should be putting into our bodies on a regular basis. These special diets have been curated to be the one-stop shop for all people and all issues. Promising to fix all your problems, they serve as a seemingly simple solution. Diets of all sorts rise and fall while attracting a plethora of consumers throughout the duration of their existence. So what *are* all these diets?

SIMPLY... A FAD

A short-term spotlight shining down on a certain diet only to be removed and replaced by the newer, shinier one—this is the fad diet regime. With ever-changing trends, it can be extremely difficult to believe whatever is in the spotlight at a certain time. Throughout it all, however, there seems to be one underlying factor: everyone trying a diet is looking to live a healthier life.

So, from this assumption, where do we go? We have determined that a better lifestyle is necessary, but there are no clear steps to easy health. Obviously, you need to work out and eat healthy to be healthy, but this isn't really mapped out in any clear manner. How does someone eat healthy? How do you work out in a healthy manner? How can you completely evolve into someone living the ideal healthy lifestyle you've set out to live?

Looking at current trends throughout American culture, we are heavily influenced by these mainstream diets—the trends that spike certain food sales, the trends that impact various industries, and the trends that lead to the creation of new restaurants. Food trends in America have a vast impact on how people live their everyday lives.

I've grown up never knowing if eggs were healthy. Some days they were, some days they weren't. I wasn't up to speed on the most recent research, so my knowledge came purely from whatever my mom had heard recently. From that logic, some days they were healthy. Other days only the whites were healthy. The public perception of food can certainly change how companies operate entirely.

As for macro trends in the United States, companies have worked to capture value from these variations in customer preferences. Different restaurants have implemented avocado or kale additions to their menu—two foods that have been in the spotlight recently. Additionally, new restaurants have been built on the principle of providing key nutrition based in certain diets.

These restaurants have captured an audience and converted it into profit. Entrepreneurs have snagged these fad diet opportunities and turned them into reality. Why go through a complex grocery list for specific, complex items when there is a restaurant that knows exactly how to make the food essential to *your* diet? The branding is based on the lifestyle you're attempting to live, and the food actually tastes good.

Companies have worked to infiltrate this niche market of fad diets. While there is a major gamble here, many of these companies have done well. If such diet falls out of the public eye, however, there may be chaos.

Working to counteract this, restaurants have worked to specialize in their field and sell their target market on the overall lifestyle involved in a value proposition.

JUICE PRESS

Millions of American worry about what they eat. What about what we drink, though?

The fresh, healthy diets that we focus on allow us to think we are being healthy. We often forget that drinks contain immense amounts of calories, and these calories can add up extremely quickly.

While a drink contains calories, it can also contain nutrients. Diets have been created to revolve around this simple shift in the state of food.

The juice diet—a seeming fad diet—has been introduced as a healthy way to lose weight and obtain key nutrients to live a better life. Companies have clearly attempted to capitalize on this: Jamba Juice, Smoothie King, Juice Stop, Juice Press, and many more have worked to provide customers with "healthy" drinks to fulfill their needs.

When looking at one company's efforts, we see that it has positioned itself in a similar manner as other ultra-health-focused restaurants. As per Juice Press' website:

> *Juice Press is on a mission to create the most trusted nutrition and wellness brand on the planet. Founded in 2010 with the vision of bringing a healthier, more transparent lifestyle platform to the market, we offer an expansive USDA organic product line as well as a variety of lifestyle resources. In seven short years, Juice Press has opened more than 70+ retail stores and is now recognized as THE premiere organic "grab and go" health food provider.*[38]

---

38 "About Us." *Juice Press.* Accessed April 07, 2019. https://juicepress.com/about-us/.

Health with transparency has clearly dominated the growing division of the restaurant industry in recent years. Yet the growth in crazy diets, such as a pure juice diet, is certainly in question.

* * *

Juice Press founder Marcus Antebi started his company after leaving his Thai boxing career.

"I was unable to find a commercial enterprise that really connected with me — [a company] that did everything, convenience, price point, organics, the formula selection, and this was an idea that was in the back of my head for at least a decade," Antebi recounted.[39]

Like many, he wanted to get behind something that he was truly passionate about—and Antebi is certainly passionate about this.

He believes the juice diet is extremely beneficial. While there are certain precautions to the madness, he believes there are evident health benefits to juice-cleansing diets.

---

39 "Interview with Marcus Antebi - Founder of Juice Press." You-Tube video, 5:34. "New to the Street," November 20, 2014. https://youtu.be/ksCIqAKGBUY.

Antebi mentioned in an interview that "it's all about choosing the juices that work best for you. And, with over 50 different ones to choose from, Marcus [Antebi] has anticipated nearly every allergy and taste. As he sees it, the juices being added to your diet are less important than the bad-for-you foods you remove."[40] There is a general consensus that you should remove the unhealthy, processed foods from your diet. This is where Marcus Antebi's Juice Press comes into play.

* * *

The juice-cleansing diet: no food, only juice.

To juice cleanse, you must undergo a set time without eating any food. The only thing you consume is juice from a pure state, which means foods from a solid state to a liquid state— and nothing in between. No randomly added unhealthy factors, but simply healthy components squeezed together to produce a liquid state of the product.

I've never tried this before, but many first-hand accounts remain the same.

---

40 Minehan, Katie. "Marcus Antebi - Juice Press Founder Interview." Marcus Antebi - Juice Press Founder Interview. March 8, 2014. Accessed April 07, 2019. https://www.refinery29.com/en-us/marcus-antebi-juice-press.

You begin to feel sick pretty quickly. This the body literally eating away at itself. *Autolysis* is the technical term for this process.

While it's a scary thought, Juice Press' founder believes that "the body has infinite wisdom not to eat vital organs, the nervous system, the brain...the body's going to go through morbid tissue, abscesses, tumors, dead cells, dying cells."[41] Antebi describes it as the body entering a healing process, which works to cleanse the body of less-desired aspects while leaving the functional and essential aspects of the body.

This "healing process" is the real driver for the diet. People are looking to be healthy—often by losing weight—and not eating will lead to quick weight loss.

Companies have attempted to capitalize on this desire in order to better fulfill consumers' goal: health. This is where many ultra-health-focused companies of the future come in.

As for Marcus Antebi, he believes that the juicing fad diet has altered the way the food industry operates.

"We're at a time in history where this is a whole new category, and anybody that has the retail experience, the product

_____

41   Ibid

experience, and the hard work ethic, they're going to prosper because the consumer in mass wants this product," Antebi explained. In the near future, he predicted, "You'll remember a time when there was a fad with juice bars, but it won't actually be like that in a decade. It'll be juice bars everywhere."[42]

Marcus Antebi has taken the bet on juice bars and their future success.

"I don't want HPP [high-pressure processed] juice; I want organic produce; I want a wide selection; I want a lot of service; and I want all the conveniences that a big brand would bring to the table," Antebi emphasized.[43]

The shift toward the future health-conscious average consumer is a major bet for companies in today's market. However, with companies continuing to enter the marketspace, the desire for the average consumer to shift to a healthy, natural, organic, and sustainable meal may become a reality in the future.

Where specialty juices have become a diet all on their own, you wonder if this diet/trend will stick or simply fade away. With fad diets stirring demand, there's an opportunity in the market. How can you keep a diet around? Or, how can

---

42 Ibid
43 Ibid

you evolve with a diet fading away? These are questions that Juice Press will be pressed with in the future.

ZOE'S KITCHEN

According to the U.S. News & World Report:

> *It's generally accepted that the folks in countries bordering the Mediterranean Sea live longer and suffer less than most Americans from cancer and cardiovascular ailments. The not-so-surprising secret is an active lifestyle, weight control, and a diet low in red meat, sugar and saturated fat and high in produce, nuts and other healthful foods. The Mediterranean Diet may offer a host of health benefits, including weight loss, heart and brain health, cancer prevention, and diabetes prevention and control. By following the Mediterranean Diet, you could also keep that weight off while avoiding chronic disease.*[44]

Living a nutritional lifestyle based off the Mediterranean diet has various health benefits, which has led to vast public appeal. Those looking to live a healthy lifestyle, lose weight,

---

44 "Best Diets Overall." *U.S. News & World Report*. Accessed April 07, 2019. https://health.usnews.com/best-diet/mediterranean-diet.

or for numerous other reasons have the ability to integrate the Mediterranean diet into their life.

With such a strong backing, the Mediterranean diet seems like the clear path to success. While this diet appears more as a lifestyle change than a short-term fad diet, the key take-aways are quite similar. Shown on the U.S. News & World Report's scorecard for diets, short-term and long-term weight loss, how easy the diet is to follow, and the actual healthiness of the diet are all accounted for.[45] These broad categories cover a majority of people interested in changing their life-style habits to a diet similar to the Mediterranean diet.

The number-one ranked diet in 2019, the Mediterranean diet has made further headway than just a typical guide on how to eat. While consumers have eaten up these fancy diets, companies have been able to capitalize; likewise, meeting the Mediterranean diet-eating customer halfway, Zoë's Kitchen operates as a fast-casual Mediterranean restaurant.

* * *

Zoë's Kitchen, based in Plano, Texas, looks to help those working to eat healthy and live a healthy lifestyle—on the Mediterranean diet or not.

---

45   Ibid

The company operates nationwide under the leadership of its parent company, CAVA. With consumer trends accepting this healthy diet, Zoë's Kitchen has been able to fill customers' desires by offering healthy Mediterranean meals.

These meals include various sandwiches, kabobs, soups and salads, and pitas. Additionally, Zoë's Kitchen offers family dinners, where the order can be made family-style instead of individual orders. Meals here look to promote the benefits of incorporating the Mediterranean diet into an everyday American life.

* * *

As chef Antonio Iocchi, vice president of food and beverage innovation, described, "[his] goal is to serve the flavors and benefits of Mediterranean cuisine to those looking for satisfying, wholesome meals."[46]

The company operates around their core values of serving healthy Mediterranean food.

---

46 "Resolutions Done Right." *Zoës Kitchen*. Accessed April 07, 2019. https://zoeskitchen.com/.

"I think what's core to us is that we're very different. Mediterranean concept," former CEO Kevin Miles explained.[47] "There's not many out there. And if they are, they're mostly local mom-and-pop concepts across the U.S. So, a very differentiated brand. It's on trend with what the customers looking for. I think just recently a Wall Street Journal talked about eating Mediterranean, living Mediterranean, and that's really what Zoë's is all about."[48]

"What's different about Zoë's is that we're a lifestyle brand," Miles elaborated.[49] "We are one of those brands that connect with the consumers in motions and attitudes, and it's really resonating across better-for-you options — great lean proteins, fresh vegetables — in a fast-casual environment.'"[50]

* * *

In order to continue success, however, the company has fearlessly innovated. As Miles, former president and CEO of Zoë's Kitchen, referenced, the brand has worked to include

---

47 "Zoe's Kitchen CEO: Differentiated Brand." *CNBC*. May 18, 2015. Accessed April 07, 2019. https://www.cnbc.com/video/2015/05/18/ zoes-kitchen-ceo-differentiated-brand-.html.

48 Ibid

49 "What's Different about Zoës Kitchen." *CNBC*. September 02, 2014. Accessed April 07, 2019. https://www.cnbc.com/video/2014/09/02/whats-different-about-zos-kitchen.html?&qsearch-term=ZOES.

50 Ibid

healthier beverages. Specifically, according to *Nation's Restaurant News*, "the drinks include kombucha, cold-brew coffee, tangerine and turmeric fresca, a fig and vanilla cooler, a blackberry-mint refresher, and hibiscus *karkadé* tea. For adult beverages, the new unit offers wines and beers on tap as well as made-to-order Moroccan sangria."[51]

As stated, Zoë's Kitchen is much more than a simple diet. It reached out and became a lifestyle brand for many of its customers. The way of life, living along with the Mediterranean diet, has become much larger than a simple lunch, dinner, or dessert menu.

While working to follow a diet—in this case the Mediterranean diet—people often have a difficult time adjusting to the lifestyle it requires. More and more companies are trying to ease this transition, however.

The common issues like "I don't want to cook tonight" and "what other kind of food can I even eat on this diet" are solved through these niche restaurants.

---

51 Ruggless, Ron. "Zoe's Kitchen Debuts Next-generation Design." *Nation's Restaurant News*. January 16, 2018. Accessed April 07, 2019. https://www.nrn.com/marketing/zoe-s-kitchen-debuts-next-generation-design.

For a company to reach out and provide unique meals, it has built up an advantage over standard fast food. Dining here completes a mission: to be healthy.

Fast-casual Mediterranean restaurant Zoë's Kitchen does a great job of providing value to its customers. With an appeal to those looking for a healthier life, it is able to successfully promote its values of serving high-quality food.

FADING DIETS

With a diet craze engulfing the masses, certain questions must be asked. Nutrition to build a healthy lifestyle has shown many faces. From that, which diets are here to stay? Which ones will disappear? How will Americans look to become healthy in the future?

By looking at just a fraction of the diets out there, we can clearly observe an internal desire for Americans to become healthier.

Americans don't want to simply work out or eat a healthy meal. Instead, they want lifestyle changes that make them feel accomplished. Food that pushes them to new beginnings. A mindset that allows them to reach goals. While certain diets quickly fall out of the public eye, a new trend is here to stay.

Healthy living, for example—healthy living is here to stay. Even with traditional, unhealthy fast-food restaurants in the market, new health-branded QSRs will begin to form for the consumer that is looking for these sorts of companies. Trends will continue to promote the healthy lifestyle as more Americans understand the impact food has on their overall life.

In conjunction with the obesity epidemic we are experiencing in the United States, more knowledge will be shared on the importance of maintaining health on an everyday basis. These trends sparks a new marketplace—one with the fresh, clean, transparently sourced food consumers want. Here, the health and well-being of individuals will be promoted.

From these trends, a new restaurant industry will slowly be born.

TO BE MAINSTREAM'D ULTRA-HEALTH RESTAURANTS

Six o'clock in the afternoon. Dinner time. Six hours since the last meal, and no motivation to cook food at home. This dilemma calls for a quick fix.

Right now, you're probably thinking about buying some inexpensive food. Maybe from the closest fast-food location—a situation in which Americans fill their gullets with highly processed, highly unhealthy food. These meals are overflowing with calories and fat, all while lacking key nutrients to help build and maintain the human body. With many Americans eating at these locations, it is no wonder the U.S. obesity rate has continued to rise over the years.

Obesity in America has been a major concern that radiates through various issues worldwide. Beyond simple individual complications, obesity has its hand in environmental changes, societal changes, medical changes, and changes throughout the food industry.

As the weight of Americans continues to grow, there has been an effort to counteract our big problem. Restaurants have worked to add "healthy" options to their menu, stores now show the calories in their menu items, and diets have seemingly taken over the world.

Even with awareness of the obesity problem continuing to grow, however, there is much to be done. Our perception of food must be altered in order to fully promote a healthy lifestyle.

Certain companies have attempted to fill this space within the industry. Restaurants have competed to be the superior provider of all healthy alternatives. While you could go through a drive-through for an unhealthy quadruple cheeseburger and fries, such companies are trying to replace that possibility with a clean, sustainable meal of their own.

This is where the food industry is adapting new trends. The market is seemingly diverging between the typical fast-food restaurant experience and the brand-new, ultra-health-focused restaurants of the future.

* * *

This story begins with the treacherous new beginning of entering an ultra-health-focused restaurant.

"What is this place? What is an acai bowl? How do you say that? What even is quinoa? Since when is fast food so elaborate? Woah! Is my meal going to cost like twenty dollars? Everyone here is so healthy. Are they making my food right now basically from scratch? This place is actually pretty cool!"

This is the rollercoaster of emotions flowing through you as you embark on your first visit to an ultra-health-conscious restaurant. The experience almost resembles that of entering a brand-new world. The food seems familiar, but it's nothing you've really experienced. The drinks make sense, but you've never tried them. Everything is different, but understandable in the world of health-focused restaurants.

"Hey there. Can I get the chicken pesto parm bowl, please?" you patiently asked.

"Will that be all for you today?" the employee inquired with a smile.

"Yeah, that'll be it," you replied.

"Wonderful!" the friendly employee said as they quickly began personalizing your meal.

After what felt like just a few seconds, the transaction continued. You curiously handed the cashier at the end of the line a crisp ten-dollar bill and some change for your meal.

A simple transaction, but through this, a new world was unlocked.

You have finally broken into the health-conscious restaurant world, and now you're ready to try the wide variety of food that all these restaurants have to offer.

Slightly upset that any food in a fast-casual setting could be so expensive, you began to raise your expectations for the meal you just bought. You then sit down to enjoy the meal that everyone had been recommending for the past couple months.

Your first bite went just as expected, but, all of a sudden, the entire bowl of food was gone. The entire chicken pesto parmesan bowl was finished. You had just eaten 525 calories. And it was great! Each bite tasted fresh, natural, and healthy.

You just experienced your first time at an ultra-health restaurant focused on sourcing from local producers, with sustainable habits, and cutting out the unhealthy processing that usually occurs in U.S. quick-service restaurants.

First examining at a key leader in the ultra-health revolution, we turn to Sweetgreen, an ultra-health restaurant whose valuation has topped $1 billion.

SWEETGREEN

Altering the way average food is created, Sweetgreen has worked to change the restaurant industry for the better. From the normal fast-food marketplace, filled with cheeseburgers, fried food, chicken nuggets, fries, fried food, unhealthy drinks, and more fried food, Sweetgreen stepped in to revolutionize the very basis of this assessment.

Breaking the typical mold of fast food and fast-casual dining, Sweetgreen found its place in the market. Embodied in its operations, the health-conscious operation questions typical procedures of fast-food establishments. Why can't we see the food being made? Why does every single store look like somebody hit copy and paste about a billion times? Why is it all so fake?

Puzzled by the sketchy atmosphere at standard fast-food restaurants, three men set out to find a better way to eat. According to a Forbes article, "Jonathan Neman remembers being a senior at Georgetown University and the mealtime choice [was] between 'slow, expensive and boring' or 'fast, cheap and really bad for you.'"[52] This has been the previous reality of eating in the United States: often eating food that does not fulfill nutritional needs, time needs, or monetary needs. But this has since been revolutionized since.

"We're creating a brand that stands for something," Co-CEO Nathaniel Ru explained. "We want to feed more people better food."[53]

Nathaniel Ru, Nicolas Jammet, and Jonathan Neman have created this billion-dollar valued company—Sweetgreen.

52 Bertoni, Steven. "PODCAST: Sweetgreen Cofounder Jonathan Neman On Turning Salad Into A Lifestyle." *Forbes*. July 24, 2018. Accessed April 07, 2019. https://www.forbes.com/sites/stevenbertoni/2018/07/24/podcast-sweetgreen-cofounder-jonathan-neman-on-turning-salad-into-a-lifestyle/#1738d9001766.

53 Kowitt, Beth. "How Sweetgreen's Co-Founders Are Creating a New Model for Fast Food." *Fortune*. February 18, 2016. Accessed April 07, 2019. http://fortune.com/2016/02/18/sweetgreen-entrepreneurs/.

From here, the standard operations for a fast-food company had been changed forever. The company is not typical, and does not aim to be so.

"What's cool is that the menu is different in all the different cities and it changes five times a year. So, to be a brand that's nationwide that has food that's different everywhere and changes differently everywhere, that's what's really exciting," Co-CEO Jonathan Neman said.[54]

Sweetgreen continues to evolve through this structure. Where standard fast-food restaurants operate using a regular menu, Sweetgreen rolls out specialty meals five times a year, as stated. From this, Sweetgreen is able to ensure its commitment to quality as it works directly with its suppliers before even determining what new meals to sell.

"Ru says that Sweetgreen will meet the farmers in a new region before meeting its landlords, since the company needs to figure out if it can create a supply chain before opening a cluster of stores," according to an article from *Business Insider*.[55]

---

54 Ibid

55 Baer, Drake. "This Trendy Salad Bar's Design Secrets Keep Customers Coming Back for More." *Business Insider*. March 21, 2016. Accessed April 07, 2019. https://www.businessinsider.com/sweetgreen-founder-interview-nathaniel-ru-2016-3.

Simple actions here illustrate the continued commitment to fresh ingredients. Since Sweetgreen is not already established nationwide, unlike the fast food behemoths discussed earlier, it must be extremely careful in its operations to maintain its core values. Promoted on its website, its core values are as follows:

- *Win, win, win — create solutions where the company wins, the customer wins, the community wins.*
- *Think sustainably — make decisions that last longer than you will.*
- *Keep it real — cultivate authentic food and relationships.*
- *Add the sweet touch — create meaningful connections every day.*
- *Make an impact — leave people better than you found them.*
- *Live the sweetlife — celebrate your passion and your purpose.*[56]

As the company continues to expand into new markets, Sweetgreen has shown a commitment to ensuring that these core values are followed. Its entire value package must be presented to every customer at every store.

This commitment is all for you, the customer.

---

56 "Our Story." *Sweetgreen*. Accessed April 07, 2019. https://www. sweetgreen.com/our-story/.

"Walking into a Sweetgreen is kind of like visiting an Apple store — with all those clean lines and smiling faces, there's a sense of relief at patronizing a retailer that feels good to visit," Nathaniel Ru said, calling this "service design."[57] By building an environment that Sweetgreen's customers can relate to and enjoy, the company has been able to capture the full essence of its core values.

Similar to a trip to Disney World, everything should be treated as an experience.

"You get in line, which Ru says should be about a 15-minute wait. When it's time to order, you stand in front of a row of ingredients, similar to Chipotle. A team member walks you through the entire process. It's one-one-one rather than an assembly line process — a change Sweetgreen made a year and a half ago. It takes a little more time but improves accuracy. From start to finish, the ordering process should take two to three minutes," *Business Insider* described.[58] The process is simple and understandable but allows for an entirely added element that other restaurants miss.

---

57 Baer, Drake. "This Trendy Salad Bar's Design Secrets Keep Customers Coming Back for More." *Business Insider*. March 21, 2016. Accessed April 07, 2019. https://www.businessinsider.com/sweetgreen-founder-interview-nathaniel-ru-2016-3.

58 Ibid

As for Sweetgreen's operations, the business eliminates a division between the consumer and the seller. The food is intertwined with the experience. With the food out on display, it's like a lot of new cars. Shown for its beautiful appearance, the green vegetables Sweetgreen sells can entice customers far more than the hidden frozen cheeseburger in the back of a shady fast food restaurant. Lucky for us, there is no car salesman pushing us to eat more food.

Adding to the experience, however, are the continual advancements to the online marketplace for the ultra-health restaurant. According to *Business Insider*, "Sweetgreen wanted the app to mimic the store experience, Ru says, so it spent a lot of time on food photography. Big images of the ingredients you can get in-store make it a more visual experience than just checking boxes. And once you order, you skip the line and go to a designated pickup area."[59]

While online orders have been expanding with the recent successes of numerous firms entering the marketspace, Sweetgreen has seen its investments pay off. Neman stated that Sweetgreen receives 50 percent through its mobile app.[60] With a shift in how consumers purchase their meals,

---

59 Ibid
60 Johnson, Eric. "Why Sweetgreen Thinks like a Tech Company." *Recode*. December 17, 2018. Accessed April 07, 2019. https://www.recode.net/2018/12/17/18144250/

companies must stay aware of this and shift toward a more technological approach. With an app that promotes the consumption of Sweetgreen, the company can expect continued growth through online app orders.

Times are a-changin'—Sweetgreen demonstrates this clearly. You no longer need to wait for food like you once did. Now, food is ready when you need it—when you *want* it. There are no lines, because you don't even need to wait! Food can be ordered from home and picked up with as little interaction as possible.

As for a shift in food service, we can expect this trend to continue. According to recode.com, Neman "envisioned a network of 'ghost and virtual kitchens' that would prepare items for rapid delivery, without a public-facing storefront."[61] This fully integrates the online orders, the nutritional health vision, speed, and the consumers accessibility. While human trends continue to change, we can expect to see Sweetgreen work to capitalize on certain characteristics that will set it apart from the standard competition in the QSR market.

As Sweetgreen continues to evolve to meet current consumer trends, other companies have taken an approach of

---

sweetgreen-jonathan-neman-fast-food-salad-delivery-block-chain-kara-swisher-decode-podcast.

61 Ibid

revolutionizing QSR operations. Sweetgreen has looked to make food quickly accessible through technology advancements and understandable operations, but not all companies in the marketplace have worked toward the goals. Another QSR working to create success has slowed down the process to add value to its consumers.

DIG INN

To "change the game."

Dig Inn's mission stands remarkably similar to other ultra-health-inspired restaurants.

"Every decision we make at Dig Inn starts with a deep respect for our ingredients and where they come from. Our recipe development process always involves a conversation between chef and grower about what we really want to cook and harvest. We work one-on-one with 102 farmers and partners to bring those recipes to life, planning crops specifically for our menus," Dig Inn's website pronounces.[62]

The company clearly illustrated its commitment to ingredients and the fresh, farm-to-table menu the restaurant revolves around.

---

62 "Our Mission." *Dig Inn*. Accessed April 07, 2019. https://www.diginn.com/mission/.

"We buy from minority-run and small-scale farms, using our purchasing power to support sustainable growing practices and invest in the future of farming," its website declares.[63]

Dig Inn appeals to its ideal customer in this statement. While many newer health companies are practicing farm-to-table operations with sustainable methods, Dig Inn takes it one step further. By illustrating its use of minority-run and small-scale farms, it makes you picture, in theory, the local community your purchases help. This continues to build the brand image. Dig Inn has taken a different approach than many to captivating the ultra-health-focused field.

"Dig Inn's core Millennial consumer is ready for a new kind of dining experience—and, no, it's not app-fast delivery or swipe-and-click ordering. Instead, [Dig Inn owner Adam] Eskin and his team see a need for another element: to slow down," according to *Forbes*.[64] In a market where firms are implementing vast amount of technology, Dig Inn has decided to differentiate themselves. Targeting millennials specifically, the firm believes there is an opportunity to branch away from speed and technology.

---

63   Ibid
64   Paul, Eve Turow. "Dig Inn Slows Down Its Quick Service Model." *Forbes*. January 11, 2017. Accessed April 07, 2019. https://www.forbes.com/sites/eveturowpaul/2017/01/11/dig-inn-runs-from-quick-service/#580051b51684.

"I really wouldn't characterize the restaurants that we're building now as fast-casual, anymore," Eskin said.[65] "We are really looking to deliver full service for the modern consumer."[66] This full-service option, however, is still issued through a fast-casual approach. While changes are being made to set the firm apart from other businesses similar in product, Dig Inn has still used a very familiar approach for service.

As I have dined at Dig Inn, the approach does remain extremely familiar. The experience going through the line and paying at the checkout counter is relatively uniform across many companies, but Dig Inn's food is the real differentiator.

After trying the "Classic Dig" bowl, I was hooked. It was filled with juicy chicken, tasty broccoli, sweet potatoes, and brown rice, and I was in awe at the meal I had purchased.

"I think there is a mindset and a thinking from before of how things get done and what happens in the food space and what happens in food service. The way we are thinking and what we want to achieve in terms of changing the way that people eat, affordably, doesn't really comport with how things used to be," Eskin reflected.[67] Dig Inn, through

---

65 Ibid

66 Ibid

67 Clifford, Catherine. "Dig Inn Founder: 'I Wouldn't Let People Tell You That You Can't Do Things'." *Entrepreneur.* September

its differentiation, has determined that it will alter the way food service is handled. Changing operations, simply shown through their corporate owned farm, demonstrates its commitment to implementing these changes.

Dig Inn has used a strategic approach of vertically integrating its supply chain. As Eskin put it, "what if not taking these tiny, drought effected cauliflower means that they're just going to double the price of squash on the next delivery? For us, that never happens. And the reason why is these relationships we've built, they're built with both parties really expressing vulnerability."[68]

Eskin uses vulnerability to make genuine connections with the people he works with. By being vulnerable with Dig Inn's suppliers, he has changed the way standard relationships operate for his business. He keeps open communication between all stakeholders at Dig Inn to allow the firm to stay operable.

Changing market conditions have the power to alter the way the food industry supplies food. Eskin, in his TEDx Talk "Fast Food Revolution," described numerous instances when

26, 2014. Accessed April 07, 2019. https://www.entrepreneur.com/video/237836.

68   "Vulnerability Is the New Black | Adam Eskin | Change Food Fest." YouTube video, 8:09. "Change Food," December 23, 2016. https://youtu.be/8Qwx3IToOpg.

food undergoes a sort of revolution and is changed, for better or for worse.[69] Where consumers desire a change in their average lifestyle, food stands to be at the forefront of what evolves. He discusses McDonald's making food accessible, Whole Foods making food healthy, and now Dig Inn working to initiate its mark on the food industry.

To build this lasting mark on the food industry, Eskin has approached supply-chain operations with a more human-centric style. Eskin explained the current situation in most supply-chain operations where "the farmers are having a tough time and he or she is the one getting the shaft, right? They're doing all the hard work, and it is really hard work! And they're often not making that much money, but everyone else along the supply chain is."[70] Dig Inn doesn't believe that the current situation is fair. Thus Eskin is creating what he calls "win, win, win, win, win" situations in which he talks to farmers and they, together, sort out the farm-to-table logistics of Dig Inn's menu offerings.

---

69 "Fast Food Revolution | Adam Eskin | TEDxBinghamtonUniversity." YouTube video, 18:08. "TEDx Talks," March 27, 2015. https://youtu.be/NMT7ulSKxog?list=PL4axzonXAvkyjwepMfoI8sn1g-1jy2pWx3.

70 Clifford, Catherine. "Dig Inn Founder: 'I Wouldn't Let People Tell You That You Can't Do Things'." *Entrepreneur*. September 26, 2014. Accessed April 07, 2019. https://www.entrepreneur.com/video/237836.

Moving forward, Eskin recognizes the need for an understanding between the complexity of the retail operations of Dig Inn locations and the farming operations that make the restaurant operable.[71] He also believes, however, that his renovated supply-chain operations can be scaled effectively. As he said, "the way we look at it, it's still just food. We don't need to put a person on the moon."[72] Food can be simple. For Dig Inn, simple may just be the key for scaling the business's model.

* * *

Eskin's beliefs about the future of the food industry require a great deal of innovation. Standard, unhealthy restaurants must change or die out, as he suggests, but new markets are opening for people to step in and fill the food void.[73] To achieve a pinnacle of influence in the future, Dig Inn has worked to structure its operations to revolutionize its company relationships. This would in turn promote its supply-chain successes beyond its current state. Through these successful changes in supply-chain operations, Dig Inn looks to bring healthy, financially responsible food to everyone.

---

71 Ibid

72 Ibid

73 "Fast Food Revolution | Adam Eskin | TEDxBinghamtonUniversity." YouTube video, 18:08. "TEDx Talks," March 27, 2015. https://youtu.be/NMT7ulSKxog?list=PL4axzonXAvkyjwepMfoI8sn1g-1jy2pWx3.

CHOPT CREATIVE SALAD COMPANY

Continuing in search of a great-tasting, healthy salad, we follow the journey here.

Before the founding of Chopt Creative Salad Company, no one had really specialized in salad. Of course, there were lame fast-food side salads and "healthy" salad options all over the United States, but no one had actually specialized in salad. It was like no one knew what they were doing!

The founder of Chopt Creative Salad Co., Tony Shure, found that "Americans love a specialist … it seemed like Americans wanted convenience and they put their faith in specialists. And we thought that if we went to the end of the earth on effort for every aspect of salad, that we would have a chance at surviving."[74]

The gutsy decision to launch a salad firm is exactly what Shure did. He researched and brainstormed with Colin McCabe, another founder of Chopt. From there, they opened up their first location in the heart of the world: New York, New York.

---

74 "2018 Festival Keynote - Tony Shure, Chopt - Founder Story & Problem Solution Fit." YouTube video, 3:00. "NYU Entrepreneurial Institute (Leslie eLab)," April 19, 2018. https://youtu.be/cgKq-JEGFSXM.

Jumping into Shure and McCabe's adventure, Nick Marsh joined the team. Marsh brought experience and a new perspective to the company. According to Marsh, "[he] was one of the guys who started Cosi back in 1997, in the early days of what's now called 'fast casual.' The idea was that better ingredients on better bread made a better sandwich. At the time, there wasn't really a name for that particular niche of the restaurant industry, but now there's a whole bunch of different companies evolving people's thinking about fast food."[75] Given Marsh's prior experience in the industry, and that he was a great fit for the company, Chopt Creative Salad Co. crowned him chief executive officer.

"I met Tony Shure and Colin McCabe, the founders of Chopt, right when they were opening their second restaurant," Marsh recalled.[76] "It was clear that they were the kind of passionate, creative entrepreneurs who would make building a business fun. Just as importantly, they were clearly pointed in the same direction in their vision for food. They were really some of the first guys to ask the question, 'Why can't fast, affordable food be healthy and taste great?' They opened

---

75   Garrity, Philip. "Get To Know Chop't Creative Salad Company's CEO Nick Marsh." *INC*. Accessed April 07, 2019. http://www.westchestermagazine.com/914-INC/Q4-2014/Get-To-Know-Chopt-Creative-Salad-Companys-CEO-Nick-Marsh/.

76   "What Inspires Chopt CEO Nick Marsh." *QSR Magazine*. January 13, 2017. Accessed April 07, 2019. https://www.qsrmagazine.com/start-finish-what-inspires-execs/what-inspires-chopt-ceo-nick-marsh.

Chopt in 2001, and I think the innovation was to move salads and vegetables to the center of the plate as opposed to a side dish."[77]

With strong successes for over a decade, Chopt has illustrated its ability to compete in the market. However, while it has had major achievements, it is still learning how to operate.

"At our Rye location [in Westchester County, New York], our customer base is 70 percent women, and we serve 250 kid meals a week," Marsh explained.[78] "As we move into the suburbs, a huge portion of our customer base is the mom who is busy and who is looking for an easy solution to eat healthy for herself and her kids. In response to that demand, we're rolling out a new kids menu. We're eliminating soda in the restaurant and rolling out our line of custom Chopt iced teas."[79]

The company continues to evolve as the desires of customers change. To ease the complexity of this evolution, however, Chopt has decided to keep everything under corporate management.

---

77 Ibid
78 Garrity, Philip. "Get To Know Chop't Creative Salad Company's CEO Nick Marsh." *INC.* Accessed April 07, 2019. http://www.westchestermagazine.com/914-INC/Q4-2014/Get-To-Know-Chopt-Creative-Salad-Companys-CEO-Nick-Marsh/.
79 Ibid

"We think innovation is critical in the restaurant industry today," Marsh emphasized. "Things are moving so fast in terms of people's tastes and the flavor profile people are interested in. We need flexibility to respond to that … [not being a franchise] gives us more opportunities to push boundaries. We're more nimble."[80]

By owning every operating store location, Chopt can roll out changes at a fast pace. While it may be costlier to fund every new initiative, the overall logistics have been streamlined. Decisions can be made this way without the consultation of numerous franchisees all looking to grow their own store. With simpler logistics, Chopt is able to work quickly on new actions and provide the greatest value for its customers in a timely manner.

So, when Marsh was asked what he believes is the secret to building a successful brand, he answered, "The No. 1 key in the restaurant industry is to consistently delight people. Our founder, Tony Shure, has a great line: 'We went into this business to make people happy.'"[81]

The key word is "consistently." There may be great times, and there could be bad times, but this should not be the case.

---

80 Ibid
81 Ibid

Every single visit to Chopt Creative Salad Co. is crafted to please the customer, crafted to please you.

As Marsh reminds those in the industry, "don't ever forget it's all about the food."[82] While Chopt works to make every single person who visits the restaurant happy, its salad specialization allows it to differentiate itself in the marketplace. With this, Chopt centralizes its food by promoting the healthy, cleanly sourced, and tasty meals served every single visit.

As Chopt Creative Salad Co. has specialized in unique salad creations, it has capitalized on what other restaurants often focus on as only a side. This seems to have given it a slight differentiation from other health restaurants in the marketplace. However, each health-based QSR has looked eerily similar. Moving forward, what does it all mean?

WHAT DOES IT ALL MEAN?

The companies discussed, such as Sweetgreen, Dig Inn, and Chopt Creative Salad Company, as well as the companies discussed later, such as by CHLOE. and Veggie Grill have all

---

82 "What Inspires Chopt CEO Nick Marsh." *QSR Magazine*. January 13, 2017. Accessed April 07, 2019. https://www.qsrmagazine.com/start-finish-what-inspires-execs/what-inspires-chopt-ceo-nick-marsh.

entered the food industry as of late. In fact, the eldest among these industry-leading firms was only founded in 2001.

All these companies are also much smaller in size than previously discussed food behemoths. Where McDonald's boasted over $21 billion in annual revenue in 2018, the largest health focused firm—Sweetgreen—is only valued at a fraction of this amount.[83]

However, while larger companies clearly have a greater hand in the pot, these newer QSRs are able to maneuver much faster to meet the needs of their consumers. Each company has its own story on how it influenced the food industry, specifically the fast-casual market.

Sweetgreen, for example, has expanded from coast to coast and hit a billion-dollar valuation. Dig Inn is looking to redefine the supply chain for restaurants by introducing vulnerability into the mix. And Chopt Creative Salad Co. has differentiated itself within the food industry through specialization of its premier salads.

---

83 "McDonald's Reports Fourth Quarter And Full Year 2018 Results And Quarterly Cash Dividend." *McDonald's Corporation.* Accessed May 2, 2019. https://news.mcdonalds.com/news-releases/news-release-details/mcdonalds-reports-fourth-quarter-and-full-year-2018-results-and.

Each company has added value to the industry, and each company has created a following that has driven it to success. While they might all look like duplicate restaurant models, each company has taken its own spin on the typical fast-casual restaurant.

By spinning standard operations in the industry, each firm has found its own niche characteristic. These slight differentiating factors allow many of them to operate in the same city—New York. This, in addition to the vast population and growing consumer trends, has worked favorably for these companies. As each company is able to pinpoint what sets it apart, these brands will continue to develop loyal customers who will hopefully keep going back for nutritious, sustainably sourced meals.

While these QSRs each have differentiating factors, these newer fast-casual dining influencers all have certain key components that remain the same throughout. Each company operates in a manner that can be duplicated in a new venture. Trends have seemingly evolved to this new era of food, yet there still looks to be untapped success within the industry.

The industry is known for tight competition and slim margins, but there are always innovators and creators who enter the field and pushed the boundaries. Moving beyond health, there are key trends that entrepreneurs can capitalize on to add additional value to the consumer, even in a complex marketplace.

CHAPTER SIX

DIVERSITY

———

Each year, Americans consume roughly 50 billion burgers.[84]

Food service is the go-to for a big, beautiful cheeseburger in the United States, and we eat a hell of a lot of them. Anyone from your Dad at the grill to a professional chef at a sit down restaurant may advertise the variety of burger, but a burger is a burger. Trust me: I am a huge fan of the variety of cheeseburgers, and I will personally seek out the best burger wherever I go, but at the end of the day, there are more food options out there than just a great burger.

---

84   "The Hidden Costs of Hamburgers." *PBS*. Public Broadcasting Service. August 2, 2012. Accessed March 22, 2019. https://www. pbs.org/newshour/science/the-hidden-costs-of-hamburgers.

With such a widespread monopoly on quick-service options, variation outside of a burger is limited. There is no variety. There is no diversity. We eat burgers and chicken and not much else. Most people don't go out and order the nice healthy salad when grabbing food fast. At least, I know that I don't too often.

However, like I've said, food is changing. Food diversity is changing too. As for changes in the typical QSR meal, these alterations don't stop in America. Companies are expanding operations to Europe. Where there is a demand, there is a company to serve, and that is what we'll look at now.

BY CHLOE'S

From one ultra-health focused restaurant to another, by CHLOE. marks another turning point for the food industry, as its website indicates:

> by CHLOE. aims to share delicious, wholesome, plant-based food that fuels and energizes without compromising flavor, taste or satisfaction. Our chef-driven vegan menu features locally-sourced ingredients in their most natural form to create inspired dishes, made 100% by us daily. We are passionate about feeding our customers hearty, nourishing

meals made from whole ingredients that can
have a positive impact on their overall mind,
body and health.[85]

Starting with the company's roots, celebrity chef Chloe Coscarelli teamed up with Samantha Wasser to start a new vegan-inspired restaurant, by CHLOE. The brand has had great success under the leadership of two women.[86] The coverage of female leaders shows the strength women have in leading the charge in the current food movement. While on this journey, both women have made immense headway in propelling a healthy lifestyle forward for everyone to share.

Diversity in the QSR industry works in many directions. Food is moving far beyond the standard burger, women are being empowered to lead companies, and food trends are diversifying even outside of the United States.

Food is ever-changing, but eating is ~hopefully~ forever.

* * *

85 "Redefining What It Means to Eat Well | the Story." *By CHLOE.* Accessed April 07, 2019. https://eatbychloe.com/the-story/.

86 Wasser, Samantha. "How a Partner Behind the Famous Vegan Restaurant Chain By Chloe Moved Forward After a Lawsuit, Online Harassment and a Miscarriage." *Entrepreneur.* August 29, 2018. Accessed April 07, 2019. https://www.entrepreneur.com/article/318862.

As stated on the company website, by CHLOE. is "committed to maintaining a sustainable and vegan lifestyle and actively contribute towards lowering [its] carbon footprint and preserving [the] planet's water supply through [its] animal-free menu, mindful ingredient sourcing and eco-friendly packaging."[87] By CHLOE. continues the trend of operating through sustainable efforts while focusing on the ingredients going into its meals.

The restaurant describes its goal as such: "to redefine what it means to eat well."[88] This ideology of eating well is shown through its commitment to a vegan-friendly menu.

"Eat well. Eat with purpose," the company encourages.[89]

The brand is represented through a strong statement with healthy, vegan food as its purpose. Like most restaurants, there are still the typical burger and meat offerings, but the company has added a vegan spin to everything. The entire menu is vegan, even items whose names are typically associated with meat products.

---

87 "Redefining What It Means to Eat Well | the Story." *By CHLOE.* Accessed April 07, 2019. https://eatbychloe.com/the-story/.
88 Ibid
89 Ibid

In comparison to the typical meat-eating American diet, by CHLOE. has taken an alternative approach to promote sustainability. "The chain said it actively works to lower its carbon footprint and preserve the planet's weather supply with an animal-free menu, mindful ingredient sourcing, and eco-friendly packaging," according to QSR Magazine.[90] From here, the growing popularity of sustainable diets should in theory allow for these ultra-health restaurants to take advantage of consumer preferences in the future. With known benefits of eating a vegan diet, the company calls upon others to live out the lifestyle that has been proven more environmentally sustainable.

This area is where by CHLOE. differentiates itself. While other ultra-health competitors look to better the environment, by CHLOE. curates a strategy that follows this exactly. Through the vegan operations, the company can actually curve its carbon footprint, ultimately bettering the environment.

By diversifying quick service offerings away from the typical burger, maybe we can have a positive impact on the environment.

---

90 Klein, Danny. "By Chloe Looks to Double Footprint After $31M Investment." *QSR Magazine*. April 05, 2018. Accessed April 07, 2019. https://www.qsrmagazine.com/fast-casual/chloe-looks-double-footprint-after-31m-investment.

∗ ∗ ∗

Co-founder and creative director Samantha Wasser emphasized that "the goal from day one was to bring vegan food to the masses and make it as accessible and as fun as possible."[91] This is exactly what by CHLOE. has done in expanding internationally. The desire for a health-conscious meal and atmosphere is not localized in the United States. Instead, there is a demand for this restaurant model in other areas of the world.

While many niche restaurants stay relatively local and in the United States, by CHLOE. has not followed this strategy. By CHLOE. has already opened an international location in London, and "the global expansion will continue throughout Europe and the Middle East, with more stores planned for London and Dubai," according to Marketwatch.[92] The brand has is challenging any notion that a vegan restaurant is only sustainable in the United States. By CHLOE. is fully bringing its cause to the masses, and not only those in America.

---

91 Settembre, Jeanette. "EXCLUSIVE: By CHLOE, the Vegan Shake Shack, Receives $31 Million Investment to Expand Globally." *MarketWatch*. April 05, 2018. Accessed April 07, 2019. https://www.marketwatch.com/story/exclusive-by-chloe-the-vegan-shake-shack-receives-31-million-investment-to-expand-globally-2018-04-05-8882611.

92 Ibid

The United States has an ever-growing obesity epidemic, but we are not the only country looking for healthy food options. Sustainable eating habits will be a growing discussion as our world faces growing environmental concerns. Outside of the standard burger joint, there is a new food movement occurring right before our eyes.

With by CHLOE. expanding, there seems to be the possibility of the world working together to limit the environmental footprint that modern nutritional habits cause and diversify the QSR industry. By CHLOE.'s expansion has proven that health trends are not confined to the United States. The world is looking for well-crafted brands that provide quality, healthy food, especially those outside of the go-to burger.

TO IMPOSSIBLE AND BEYOND

In a world where food sourcing is becoming ever more of an issue, people must examine where their food is coming from. Companies such as Impossible and Beyond Meat have looked toward sustainably sourced "meat" products. These are typical meat items, such as burgers and sausage, that don't actually contain any meat. However, they do carry the same—or at least a very similar—texture and taste.

While this may sound crazy, it is heating up.

Companies such as Burger King and other major fast food players are looking to partner with these companies to appeal to the environmentally and health-conscious consumer. Burger King is now selling its very own Impossible Whopper at select stores, and many companies have already began selling their own meatless alternatives.

But why?

Meat and dairy consumption in the United States produces 60 percent of the greenhouses gases released from agriculture.[93] The processes behind the scene significantly affect the world we live in. Given this major issue, we are seeking solutions. Our typical diet is slowly destroying the planet. By moving to a more sustainable diet, we can cut down on our greenhouse gas emissions.

"A vegan diet is probably the single biggest way to reduce your impact on planet Earth, not just greenhouse gases, but global acidification, eutrophication, land use and water use," explained University of Oxford Ph.D. student Joseph Poore.[94]

---

93   Carrington, Damian. 2018. "Avoiding Meat and Dairy Is 'Single Biggest Way' to Reduce Your Impact on Earth." *The Guardian.* May 31, 2018. https://www.theguardian.com/environment/2018/may/31/avoiding-meat-and-dairy-is-single-biggest-way-to-reduce-your-impact-on-earth.

94   Ibid

There are solutions to the serious issues we face, and companies are now starting to shift toward building them. While not all people may buy into the vegan diet, cutting down on the 50 billion burgers in the United States and switching them out with an alternative will push us one step in the right direction.

CHAPTER SEVEN

SAFETY

The Centers for Disease Control and Prevention (CDC) have issued a new report that romaine lettuce should not be eaten in America at this time.

The CDC has issued a new report.

The CDC says you should avoid eating X at this time. The CDC says... The CDC says...

What is going on?

* * *

Like a typical American, I eat a lot of food, a lot of the time. However, unlike many Americans, I haven't yet gotten sick from eating contaminated food—luckily. According to the CDC, one in six Americans each year do actually get sick from eating contaminated food.[95]

We hear about it and see it everywhere, but we always hope we are on the right side of the fork when it does actually happen. The question still remains, though: what is going on?

While many major companies in the food industry have had encounters with food safety issues, I will focus on a key player that has experienced numerous difficulties in the past few years: Chipotle Mexican Grill.

FOOD FIRST, ALWAYS?

Chipotle has faced major problems throughout its history. After a widespread E. coli outbreak a few years back, the restaurant had to learn to recover from such a highly publicized downfall.

While attempting to learn more about how Chipotle handled this issue, I interviewed a former employee who worked on the food safety team after the E. coli outbreak—for privacy reasons, we'll call her Josie Johnson.

---

95 "Food Safety Home Page | CDC." *Centers for Disease Control and Prevention.* Accessed May 24, 2019. https://www.cdc.gov/foodsafety/index.html.

As a food safety specialist working to prevent future out-breaks at Chipotle, Johnson helped add new procedures to ensure the safety of customers and, in turn, the brand. While Chipotle has experienced significant success as a restaurant, it had to reaffirm its commitment to customers post-food-borne outbreak to rebuild the Chipotle brand.

During Johnson's time at Chipotle, she worked to answer one important question: how do we get a team on the front lines to really care about food safety?

Johnson told me that, while explaining a task to prevent food-borne illnesses, "employees are told to check the temperature of the food, but there is a difference between putting the thermometer in the right spot to see if the food is hot enough to kill possible foodborne pathogens or if the thermometer is just in the hottest spot where workers know that it will be a certain temperature."

She discussed how this issue can impact operations and explained that there is a necessity to build a "culture of food safety" because of various benefits of doing so. She looked at how integrating the new procedural culture would affect employees. The idea was to allow employees to feel a sense of accomplishment while working. By producing and sell-ing healthy, uncontaminated food, workers would be able to feel proud for the work they're contributing. And, as

Johnson mentioned, a typical Chipotle worker is also a Chipotle customer.

"The food is great. I ate so much Chipotle this summer it's ridiculous," Johnson said jokingly.

Even those who work at Chipotle eat at Chipotle—which ideally encourages employees to be even more aware of food safety procedures. If employees understand the value they are providing, they may feel obligated to provide high-quality service to Chipotle's customer base.

Moreover, an aspect Johnson discussed further was the product specification and safety plan that Chipotle locations need to follow. The supply-chain staff works together to create a clean, consistent, and operational path in order to ensure firm success. Beyond this, Johnson has looked at how safety plans can be enforced and followed strictly, so foodborne illnesses are not passed on to the consumer.

As they work to ensure these overarching food safety initiatives are followed, Johnson believes managers should not punish workers for doing the wrong thing. She mentioned that this leads to a culture of cheating responsibilities while attempting to maintain food standards.

For all food operations, providing safe food is the most important aspect of operation. If a customer gets sick, everyone in the establishment has failed to adequately do their job. In the future, QSRs must work to ensure their food safety plans are followed.

* * *

Continuing with Chipotle specifically, its ingredients have always been a focal point of its business. Since its founder came from a culinary background, Chipotle originally put quality at the forefront of its operations, with the idea of making and serving great food. And while this has certainly contributed to receiving great-tasting food, it stands as a roadblock moving forward.

Since the various issues Chipotle has recently faced, employees believe Chipotle has been paying for it dearly. Staffers have been held under tight regulation, investors have been on a rollercoaster ride, and corporate management has had to make tough decisions.

The outbreaks in Chipotle's past have put the fast-casual Mexican restaurant in the spotlight, thus management has had to make key decisions to keep the brand afloat. An example of this is the release of Chipotle's queso. While working to temper the loss from the foodborne illness outbreak, Chipotle quickly launched its own queso. The product was created to help earnings but lacked the quality other Chipotle products had.

In terms of Chipotle's recent operations, however, the new CEO has put investors' interests over the quality of ingredients, a major shift from Chipotle's founding. The queso addition illustrates this shift in management. Moving forward, however, Chipotle must actively enforce its food safety precautions to ensure that future outbreaks are nonexistent. Providing safe food should be Chipotle's first priority.

To manage this, however, putting food first might not be the best action plan. Instead, Chipotle should look to its workers to help build the company. As many are loyal Chipotle customers themselves, the fast-casual Mexican restaurant should work to leverage this.

In the long run, though, Chipotle seems set up very well to rebound from its past issues with E. coli. By maintaining a commitment to improve on various fronts, Chipotle has drastically improved and will continue to do so. However, as the restaurant has found its own way to differentiate itself in a crowded industry, other QSRs have also found their own way to stand out in the competitive marketplace.

CHAPTER EIGHT

CONVENIENCE

While many Americans have a relatively convenient place to buy food, getting food to a convenient place for the consumer really *isn't* that convenient; in fact, "it is estimated that the meals in the United States travel about 1,500 miles to get from farm to plate," according to the Center for Urban Education about Sustainable Agriculture.[96] This means the consumers' convenience does not equate to what's convenient for everyone involved. Instead, our food system relies on complex distribution networks that span the globe.

That being said, however, most consumers don't really care. If our food tastes good, is healthy, and looks fresh, we don't

---

96 "How Far Does Your Food Travel to Get to Your Plate?" *CUESA*. February 5, 2018. Accessed May 24, 2019. https://cuesa.org/learn/how-far-does-your-food-travel-get-your-plate.

bat an eye. While this raises many more questions about sustainability and food's impact on the environment, we will focus on convenience now and look at the greater effects later on. For now, we should examine exactly how convenient food really is for the consumer and where the food industry is headed in terms of consumer convenience.

* * *

"Hey. I just ordered our food. It should be here in about an hour or so."

"Sounds great! What'd you get?"

"Oh, I just got a large pizza using Uber Eats."

* * *

Food delivery is rapidly changing with the expansion of newer services. Just a few years ago, only select restaurants delivered, and platforms like UberEats, GrubHub, Postmates, and all sorts of others were either limited in scope or didn't even exist.

Now, however, food delivery is easy. Your phone holds the key to quick meals without having to leave the comfort of wherever you are.

Food delivery is growing faster than ever, too. Changes here are also heavily led by young adults, with 63 percent of individuals 18 to 29 years old ordering from a multi-restaurant food delivery app.[97] This is certainly a unique industry.

From my own experience as a college student, I have used various food-delivery services. The late-night study sessions are often matched with a delivery driver and a hot meal right at the library. Other nights, however, I stay comfortable in bed and order a nice meal as I binge-watch hours of Netflix, while procrastinating my work, of course. It is a balance, though.

Over the next few years, however, we are sure to see a major switch up in how we get our food. As experts attempt to quantify the future growth, the "investment bank UBS projects that online food ordering may rise more than 20% annually to $365 billion by 2030" and "analysts at Morgan Stanley believe that delivery could eventually top 40% of all restaurant sales," according to Zion & Zion, a reputable advertising agency in Arizona.[98] We can see that food-delivery services are just beginning their growth stage.

---

97 Zion, Aric, Fred Petrovsky, Jennifer Spangler, and Thomas Hollman. "Food Delivery Apps: Usage and Demographics - Winners, Losers and Laggards." *Zion and Zion*. Accessed May 24, 2019. https://www.zionandzion.com/research/food-delivery-apps-usage-and-demographics-winners-losers-and-laggards/.

98 Ibid

However, with the growth of food-delivery services, brick-and-mortar restaurants face many challenges. As quick-service restaurants—already focused on speed and convenience—look to become more convenient, these restaurants may have to alter their business model.

Furthermore, according to Zion & Zion, "some restaurants are concerned at this trend, and with good reason. Delivery by a third party can make it difficult to control customer service, food quality and branding. And while total sales may increase due to the ease of ordering, restaurants may face profitability issues. The New Yorker quoted a restaurateur who articulates these concerns: 'We know for a fact that as delivery increases, our profitability decreases,' with 20% to 40% of delivery revenue going to third-party platforms and couriers."[99]

As convenience for the consumer increases, it seems inevitable that something else must change. When Don Fox, CEO of Firehouse of America LLC, looked at the changing landscape of food service, he noticed something interesting in his stores.

"I'd be thinking, 'Boy, business must be pretty bad.' But the numbers were telling me a different story," Fox recounted.[100]

---

99 Ibid
100 Zaleski, Olivia. "Restaurants Shrink as Food Delivery Apps
    Get More Popular." *Bloomberg.* October 29, 2018. https://www.

People are still getting their food from restaurants, but they're not eating there … or even going there! Instead, food is ordered online through an app. Simple, and easy.

So, what is the impact of this new development?

Moving forward, we may see new restaurant operations pop up. Instead of large, dine-in brick-and-mortar storefronts, maybe there will just be a kitchen. Maybe a small counter to order with limited seating. Or maybe just a window to order at.

What if we don't actually need full restaurants but rather just a good kitchen and someone to deliver—how does that work then?

According to Bloomberg, "some new restaurant owners are skipping tables and chairs altogether and just leasing kitchen space to prepare food for couriers. Those are called cloud kitchens or virtual restaurants because they have no dining rooms or wait staff and sell their meals through the internet and mobile apps like DoorDash or UberEats."[101]

bloomberg.com/news/articles/2018-10-29/restaurants-shrink-as-food-delivery-apps-get-more-popular.

101 Ibid

Furthermore, Bloomberg reported, "David Orkin, who runs the U.S. restaurant division of real estate advisory firm CBRE, said other restaurants are also adjusting to fewer visitors."[102] The trend to accommodate customers' desire for convenience is not limited to newer establishments. Restaurants nationwide must adjust as "there is an overall downsizing of restaurant seating space as chains experience less foot traffic and more online and mobile-ordered pickups."[103]

With the growth of food-delivery services and the shift toward eating outside of restaurants, consumers may be leading the charge toward full-service convenience dining. Consumers may never have to leave their house to get the food they want—from any restaurant.

As many food-delivery services currently target QSRs and faster sit-down restaurants, there is no definite end to the scale that these companies may obtain. While 60 percent of customers value the speed of delivery dearly and say that they would like to wait no more than sixty minutes for their food, would things change for an eloquent meal in the comfort of your home?[104] What if five-star restaurants were to expand their operations to food delivery?

---

102 Ibid

103 Ibid

104 Hirschberg, Carsten, Alexander Rajko, Thomas Schumacher, and Martin Wrulich. "The Changing Market for Food Delivery." *McKinsey & Company.* November 2016. Accessed May 24, 2019.

This is just a hyperbole used to examine the growth of food delivery, but the real question remains what companies can do to make the most of this newer opportunity.

Who can create the most value? Who can provide the most convenient service?

Also, who can operate ethically, and who can help society in this new business era?

https://www.mckinsey.com/industries/high-tech/our-insights/the-changing-market-for-food-delivery.

CHAPTER NINE

SOCIAL CONSCIOUSNESS

You just finished your lunch—or, I guess, *most* of your lunch.

You begin by standing up while scanning for the nearest garbage can. From there, it's a simple journey. You walk over, toss everything, and you're on your way.

Wait … *wrong.*

* * *

You just finished your lunch—or, I guess, *most* of your lunch.

You begin by standing up while scanning for the nearest place to dispose of what's on your tray. From there, it's a simple journey. You walk over, put your leftover food in the compost bin, dump your liquids into a large bucket, recycle everything and anything that can be, and throw away the minimal amount that's left. And now, you're on your way.

* * *

Our planet is in big trouble, and it's our responsibility to fix it.

Our oceans, our landfills, our streets, our *world* is covered in garbage.

Food has such an impact on our planet, and we must take action.

* * *

When we look at the big picture, we can see so much that needs to be done. However, once we begin breaking down the big issue into its smaller components, we will find manageable tasks we can all help out with.

When it comes to food, the way we eat matters. The food we eat matters. How we source our food matters. Americans are overweight, and it's causing big problems. We consume more than we need, we waste more than we should, and we destroy more than we preserve. This is all coming into play now, and we must make the choice to change for the better.

The U.S. obesity epidemic and the war on climate change are two major issues that we can impact through our consumption of food. As I said, we have the ability to make a change for the better.

VEGGIE GRILL

From a young age, children often look at their plate and choose what food they would like to eat. Obviously, it's the desserts and the fried, cheesy, unhealthy food that kids really enjoy, while vegetables are largely ignored and relegated to the back seat at the dinner table. Everything else is more enjoyable than the "ewwwie"-tasting vegetables.

However, we've all got someone there telling us to eat our vegetables.

Vegetables are a key food group that nearly all of us know we should eat, yet we often don't. We still don't eat our vegetables. We've had Mom, Dad, Grandma, Grandpa, brothers, and sisters all telling us to eat our vegetables our entire lives, but we still don't get enough of them in our diet. It's an obvious solution. Just eat more vegetables. The benefits are huge!

Eyesight, strong hair, nails, preventing serious diseases, etc. With this sustainable way to improve the human body, it's no wonder why we've had family members telling us to eat vegetables our whole life. So why don't we eat them?

Attempting to take advantage of the numerous benefits of vegetables, Veggie Grill stands as another QSR riding the ultra-health conscious wave. Veggie Grill is currently in locations primarily on the West Coast; the company is branching out, however, to Chicago, New York City, and Boston in the near future.

Similar to the rest of your family, Veggie Grill is working to get you, along with everyone else, eating your vegetables. While this isn't the only thing it has on its menu, the restaurant takes pride in the freshness and quality of the namesake vegetables.

The company has used vegetables as the centerpiece of its entire business enterprise. By using vegetables as the mechanism to target people's "health radar," Veggie Grill has marketed vegetables as *the crispy conversation starters, the gooey smile filled bites, and the spicy friendship-builders.*[105]

---

105 "We See Veggies For What They Are." *Veggie Grill*. Accessed April 07, 2019. https://www.veggiegrill.com/our-story.html.

The company goes further by explaining initiatives key to its ideology. A statement like *"we cut veggies, not corners"* illustrates how committed the company is to fresh produce.[106] Explanations of their operations state that "behind each veggie-filled dish is a story that starts long before that first bite. It all begins with like-minded people we love—those who go the extra mile to grow the best ingredients out there. Once those fresh ingredients reach our kitchen, we take our time to make each dish right… That means from chopping to saucing, we are always coming up with new ways to celebrate the best of every season, bite after craveable bite. At our place, we work to make bold and innovative dishes that offer a whole new experience for your taste buds and make you feel like you've never felt before."[107] Veggie Grill pledges a commitment to quality and taste similar to various other health conscious QSRs operating nationwide.

Veggie Grill's current CEO, Steve Heeley, has some interesting insight he shared on the company. Branded as a veggie-centric establishment, Veggie Grill does not solely attract customers focused on that. As Heeley elaborated, "Interestingly enough, you know, we do attract vegans and vegetarians, but about 80 percent of our guests don't consider themselves vegan or vegetarian. They're what we call 'veggie

---

106 Ibid
107 Ibid

positive.'"[108] Being a vegan-positive restaurant doesn't have to limit a company's customer base, which Veggie Grill has demonstrated.

While many of Veggie Grill's customers are not vegan, Heeley believes that the company is "a vegan concept and always will be."[109] Following this, Heeley stated that Veggie Grill's "vegan or vegetarian guests understand that, and they depend on us for that. But I think where we come from is — we start out with 'What do our guests want to eat today?' And so, we come at it from the food first and then what we do is as we engineer it so that it's vegan. So, we do a lot of product development."[110] With an eccentric vegan focus, Veggie Grill has been successful through its customer-centric approach.

While serving vegan meals, Veggie Grill adequately promotes major issues. The foods that it sources help better the environment. Instead of producing and manufacturing many pounds of meat each year, the company sources fresh, sustainable vegetables. And instead of producing unhealthy junk food meals, Veggie Grill offers healthy options to its customers. Even if you're worried about getting sick of

108 Mills, Eliza. "Veggie Grill CEO Steve Heeley on Expansion and 'veggie Positivity'." *Marketplace.* January 6, 2017. Accessed April 07, 2019. https://www.marketplace.org/2017/01/06/business/veggie-grill-ceo-steve-heeley-expansion-and-veggie-positivity.
109 Ibid
110 Ibid

vegetables, Veggie Grill continues to innovate with its four seasonal menus.

Heeley is always asking, "What are the interesting flavors and foods that our guests are looking for, and how can we innovate and be creative and bring them things that maybe are really surprising, that they didn't know that they could get at a vegetarian restaurant?"[111]

He works to broaden the marketspace for the vegan and vegetarian diet. When asked about his investor's openness to investment, Heely explained, "A lot of our investors really understand trend and the trend around plant-based eating especially with millennials, and the rising tide of millennial spending. Vegan and plant-base and all that, which used to be on the fringe, is now going mainstream. So, there's a lot of sort of critical mass going on around this movement to eat more plant-based items. I think over the next couple decades eating this type of a diet and this type of food is going to be more mainstream than probably a carnivorous diet today."[112]

Heeley has high aspirations for Veggie Grill. Given his predictions based on current trends in the restaurant industry, he is certainly looking to grow the company. With these

111 Ibid
112 Ibid

trends occurring nationwide, however, he is not too worried about competition.

"A lot of brands are now coming to market with better for your options. They're coming to market with a lot of vegetarian options. And we don't necessarily see that as competition," Heeley described. "We see that as widening the audience for this type of food. I think what we do is very different than some of the other brands that have vegetarian options. We consider ourselves the experts and the innovators,'" Heeley stated.[113]

With differentiation and a first-mover advantage, Veggie Grill does have a leg up on the competition. However, innovators will always be lurking. Therefore, Veggie Grill has continued to work to stay competitive. With its high-quality ingredients, the restaurant has managed to keep prices reasonable. Heeley stated that "it's challenging because we use a lot of specialty ingredients, so they naturally come in at a higher cost. And so, you know, it's always a balance of price versus quality, but we try to engineer a purchasing and supply chain, and our vendor partnerships, so that we can keep our food affordable and guests can come in a lot, and we do have a lot of highly frequent guests."[114]

---

113 Ibid
114 Ibid

Veggie Grill has been able to captivate the health-conscious consumer in the current era. Meals served here also work to alleviate problems in the United States. By mindfully sourcing our food and watching what we eat, we can make a change for the better. This is exactly what companies are doing nowadays: working for the betterment of the planet.

For Veggie Grill moving forward, innovation will continue to allow the vegan restaurant to expand and thrive. With the ability to help the environment and keep Americans healthy, it seems to be on the right path to success. As its website proudly states, *"We believe in 'more veggies, please!'"*[115]

* * *

However, to succeed, any company—not just Veggie Grill—must understand the larger trends impacting an industry. As Veggie Grill mindfully serves vegan food, its service helps promote a better world. Stated once more, Joseph Poore at the University of Oxford noted that "a vegan diet is probably the single biggest way to reduce your impact on planet Earth, not just greenhouse gases, but global acidification, eutrophication, land use and water use."[116] Therefore, by understanding

---

115 "We See Veggies For What They Are." *Veggie Grill.* Accessed April 07, 2019. https://www.veggiegrill.com/our-story.html.

116 Carrington, Damian. 2018. "Avoiding Meat and Dairy Is 'Single Biggest Way' to Reduce Your Impact on Earth." *The Guardian.* May 31, 2018. https://www.theguardian.com/environment/2018/

industry trends and how to capitalize on them, a QSR should be able to leverage opportunity to better the world.

may/31/avoiding-meat-and-dairy-is-single-biggest-way-to-reduce-your-impact-on-earth.

CHAPTER TEN

CAPTURING SUCCESS

———

If you work just for money, you'll never make it, but if you love what you're doing and you always put the customer first, success will be yours.[117]

—RAY KROC

By becoming great at something you enjoy, you will eventually find success in your path. Success is shown through many great leaders, especially in today's society. Elon Musk, for example, is a serial entrepreneur and visionary. He has said it takes eighty hours a week to make an impact on the

———

117 "Ray Kroc Quotes." *BrainyQuote*. Xplore. Accessed May 24, 2019. https://www.brainyquote.com/quotes/ray_kroc_173414.

world.[118] With Kroc's and Musk's individual contributions to society, these two have altered the daily life of millions of Americans, and many others worldwide.

So, moving forward, how do we change the world?

* * *

For those interested in competing within the rigorous landscape of the food industry, there are many essential trends that entrepreneurs cannot miss. Looking into the new world of food, healthy food specifically, consumer trends have shifted drastically. No longer does the cheapest, most unhealthy double mc-whatever burger win. No. Instead, a new wave of health has overcome a large segment of consumers.

Food plays a monumental role in the functions of our everyday lives, and people are acting on this. Beyond simply the physiological need to eat, most people really do enjoy the actual experience of eating. I know I do. This moves us to a place of competition within the food industry.

---

118 Matousek, Mark. "Elon Musk Says People Need To Work Around 80 Hours Per Week To Change The World." *Business Insider.* November 26, 2018. Accessed June 14, 2019. https://www.businessinsider.com/elon-musk-says-80-hours-per-week-needed-change-the-world-2018-11.

As Kroc prioritized the importance of holding the customer on the highest pedestal, so too must new entrants understand that this principal will remain true. *Treat the customer like family, and the value you provide, and the value given in return, will surpass that of anything imaginable.* By building value for your customer, you can increase your company's bottom line and ensure long-term sustainability for your company.

Every QSR being built now and in the future must possess an endless drive to better serve the customer. Looking specifically at McDonald's, it implements is the adaptation to consumer preferences by using cage-free eggs and rolling out new products that customers love. Other companies, however, must learn to embrace their mission statement and serve a purpose.

Putting the customer first is a major factor in today's business operations. Where a multitude of other factors influence a company, the customer is by far the most important. By pinpointing the customer's needs, and going above and beyond expectations, a QSR can build a strong foundation.

In such a competitive market as the food industry, however, companies must find a way to differentiate themselves—and actually find this outlet of support. Given this, finding a niche and excelling in an untapped segment of the industry should be a priority for entrepreneurs.

Looking briefly outside of the food industry, Apple Inc. attempts to predict customer preferences even before its customers knows what they want, adding to its reputation and value provided. Companies in the food industry can match this. By capitalizing on a niche offering, restaurants can ensure demand for their own brand is strong. There are countless restaurants making small margins off each check, but even so, there are ways to capture a piece of the pie through value-added differentiation.

As illustrated throughout this book, there are many rapidly occurring changes within the food industry. However, the entrepreneurs who will come out on top are the ones who can successfully add value to their customers' lives and differentiate themselves from the competition.

5 MAJOR TRENDS – HOW TO CAPTURE SUCCESS

HEALTH – BUILT ON BRAND

For a new firm to capture success as an ultra-health restaurant, an entrepreneur must focus on building a quality brand reputation. A new brand must be tactically designed and appeal to a certain segment of consumers.

In this case, a big question stands: *how do you want to be remembered?*

For a restaurant, a brand reputation is the long-lasting taste in the customer's mouth after they leave the restaurant. A brand will be built on the experience, the message, and the value provided. With this in mind, remember that there is only one opportunity to make a first impression.

Consumers are easily swayed and quickly moved by word of mouth. If the new enterprise builds a strong foundation of loyal customers, it is in good standing moving forward. However, if negativity flows throughout the beginning of operations, or at any point in time, then a quick change must be enacted.

That all said, it doesn't really mean much. That's the game of business, though. This is where creativity can be added. This is where differentiation can take place. This is where an entrepreneur can have fun and take risks. A brand is a lasting legacy, and a creator's personality can shine through here.

DIVERSITY – BUILT ON FOOD

To capture success as a new company, a restaurant's offerings must also be unique! As food continues to evolve, people are moving away from the typical fast-food cuisine. Now, food is moving toward more distinctive, fresh food, all while being ready to eat in a timely manner. This open-ended trend allows for new players to enter the food industry, however.

With food progressing from the burger-and-fries American diet, entrepreneurs can experiment in the kitchen and design a new menu to appeal to the new age consumer. As we have seen, restaurants have worked in sustainable, vegetarian, and vegan offerings; there are many more outlets to attack, though.

Through ever-increasing diverse offerings, new QSRs can work to differentiate themselves from the competition while specializing on a unique offering. From here, no longer is the burger-and-fries meal the go-to; instead, we get options, and we get a choice as the consumer.

SAFETY – BUILT ON RELATIONSHIPS

When establishing a QSR, founders must consider the little details involved with operations. Even though food safety certainly isn't a little detail, issues with food quality can often be overlooked and lead to major complications. For restaurants, food safety should be a priority over nearly every other operation occurring.

However, issues with food safety unfortunately don't come as an "if it happens" issue; they're more of a "when it happens" ordeal. Of course, there are steps required to limit foodborne illness; these are likely in the form of written procedures and must be followed and emphasized constantly.

To really achieve success, however, a company must care for its consumers and a relationship must be formed. This can begin through various factors, but, regarding food safety, can be shown through the cleanliness of the restaurant and the standards employees hold themselves to while at work.

This relationship that the company manages, however, should not only be held between the company and customer. Instead, a multitude of relationships must be formed to ensure food safety. Customers, employees, and the restaurant must all manage their relationships in order to cultivate the best overall outcome.

If a QSR can create meaningful relationships with their customers and employees, food safety protocols will first and foremost be followed well. After this, when issues do arise, customers may be willing to give the restaurant a second chance, but only if there is a strong commitment to the customer. By leveraging these positive relationships, a restaurant can operate at a much more reputable standard, allowing for greater future successes.

Moving forward, after an incident does occur, a restaurant must learn to better its operations. Many companies have faded away because of food-related issues, but others have learned to navigate the storm and are still successful today.

CONVENIENCE – BUILT ON OPERATIONS

To further add value for the consumer, entrepreneurs must add convenience for their customers. But for various restaurants, the notion of convenience may entail different things. As we looked at before, convenience may mean super-fast delivery services, but it may also encompass upgrades to technology and accessibility.

Convenience may include two drive-through windows instead of just one to account for the lunch rush, and it may entail various other upgrades in operations to help the end user. Given this range of possibilities, taking time to map out appropriate operations for a restaurant is necessary.

Restaurant operations should revolve around adding value to the end user while maximizing corporate utility. As mentioned earlier, however, business is built on relationships, and a restaurant should not squeeze its customers for every last dime. In any situation, understanding who the QSR is serving should be the grounding force in most decisions.

Operational decisions should be made by taking the perspective of the customer into account.

SOCIAL CONSCIOUSNESS – BUILT ON CORPORATE ETHICS

Last—but certainly not least—we must find a way to capture success through moral corporate ethics, as a company moving into fruition in today's era should be ethical in all aspects of operation.

This involves a million different viewpoints, as everyone has their own philosophy here, but overall, it can come down to a single idea: *an effort to always work toward bettering the world as a whole.* With this guiding principle, entrepreneurs can work to single handedly take us one step closer to a better world.

ALL FOR ONE, NOT ONE FOR ALL

Through these five avenues of capturing success, there is evidently some overlap. An entrepreneur cannot simply pick a single avenue on which to act; instead, each avenue must simultaneously be in play. In addition, there is not a one-size-fits-all map to success. Business is wild, and planning the actual route is part of the battle.

With five major trends, we have seen five ways to capture success; there is, however, quite a journey that an entrepreneur must take to reach the summit. The food industry is quickly changing, and there are opportunities scattered nationwide.

CHAPTER ELEVEN

THE JOURNEY

———

A day in my life: waking up to the sound of my blaring alarm, I slowly peel myself out of my bed. The standard day for a college student starts now, probably with too little sleep and what feels like too much to do. I quickly go through my morning routine getting ready for class. I jump in the shower, brush my teeth, decide what to wear, and pull myself together. Recollecting my thoughts, I run through my plans for the day and what classes I have.

I quickly finish up my last-minute homework assignments that are due later in the day and toss it all into my backpack. From here, I am off. There is one thing I forgot though: to eat. I didn't get breakfast.

I tell myself I'll just wait for lunch. Like usual.

My class finally ends, and I am starving. Thirty minutes for lunch gives me just enough time to stop by the nearest dining hall and still get to my next class on time.

I search the dining hall for the best options. Fried food, food that doesn't taste good, food that makes you ask, "*what is that?*" and everything else of that nature. I quickly settle and eat the nearest thing, then rush to my next class, half-full of unhealthy, unknown dining hall food.

Similar to my routine experience, others have gone through the same.

CHANGING PERCEPTION OF FAST FOOD

Trapped in a city without quick and easy food, and stuck with a limited ability to eat healthy food on campus, students face this reality every day. The general decision stands between maximizing cash, speed, taste, healthiness, and quality.

One student at Wake Forest, however, was not pleased with this system, like many others. However, unlike others, he wanted to solve the problem that everyday college students were facing. He was on a mission to mix up food on campus and alter the way fast food was perceived.

Jesse Konig set out on this mission while in school. He first began his entrepreneurship venture in a class at Wake Forest. His hot dog revolution began with just a simple idea: re-imagining the typical mystery meat used in the production of hotdogs, Konig worked to maneuver these stereotypes. His ideas stem from a desire to implement change.

Konig asked the simple question, "*Why is there no good food on campus that is affordable?*"

From here, his venture took off. His friends started scheming new ways to innovate. And through this process, the company Swizzler was born. Swizzler: a healthy take on the traditional hot dog. A new style, including quality ingredients, and a spiral-cut hot dog. Konig co-created Swizzler with the hope that he could generate a positive image for food that had previously been poorly manufactured by changing the food's reputation.

While founding Swizzler, Konig knew that he "wanted to make a real impact that could really help people." He wanted to turn the typical mystery meat meal into something that consumers could trust.

Given all this, though, changing the perception of fast food has not happened overnight, and there is still tons of work to be done. Swizzler started off as a low-risk food trunk operation right out of college but has been quickly expanding. From its origin, Swizzler looked to build on key principles that promoted honorable operations. Now, however, the company looks to expand from a food truck startup into a limitless restaurant operation.

"We think the bigger opportunity is to take the same negative perception on the hot dog and changing what people think about it and try to do that to fast food. Trying to expand that great sourcing, high-quality ingredients, transparency, and trust," Konig said.

* * *

Obviously, there is a bigger message than simply making a quick buck. The outcome of running a company, such as Konig's, branches far beyond the money. Swizzler looks to empower others through healthy alternatives to grill food. The company also looks at the overall impacts on the economy, the environment, and the individual.

This action is seen far beyond Swizzler, though. A changing perception regarding fast food and fast-casual dining is currently in the making, and it continues to alter the food industry. The changing perception allows for shifts within the well-established industry; from here, new players can work to make their mark.

Looking forward, changing the perception of fast food continues the current trends facing America today. As consumers are consistently looking to improve and move away from the U.S. obesity epidemic, health trends have risen to counteract this epidemic. However, this is clearly not a company-specific issue—meaning that one company cannot change this alone.

But companies are able to slowly integrate their ideology into the cultural norms of society. Companies in today's era are not solely brought up as money making machines. While that may certainly be a perk of running a business, companies are now expected to engage in some sort of corporate social responsibility and give back to communities.

By influencing the population today, companies may see that influence reflected in society tomorrow. If fast food slowly shifts from the unhealthy, fatty norm of today to a quick, healthy, stronger tomorrow, then the entire face of the industry has evolved.

To make this monumental change, one enterprise cannot do it all. But by slowly making statements, we begin the journey to a healthier future.

CHANGE IS A MARATHON

"I don't know if it's exactly true, but if you look at Tesla over there, their mission is to create an affordable, economical car that every person can drive. But, when they are doing that, they have to start with that luxury vehicle … because they couldn't afford to have a factory and keep the lights on selling $30,000 vehicles until technology got there" Jesse Konig pointed out.

Tesla started off by manufacturing really expensive cars to break into the market. Now that they have secured recognition, received capital, and created the technology necessary for success, the firm can bring prices down and sell cheaper electric cars to the general public.

In the food industry, restaurants can operate the same way. Companies must find a gap in the market to successfully penetrate the food industry. Given how competitive the industry is, this can be harder than it sounds, though.

Konig mentioned the strategic game that QSRs can engage in to compete fiercely. Companies can price certain items at a loss while earning profits from higher margin items. Within the highly competitive food industry, competition is brutal—and it looks even more daunting when you consider the size of many key players. For new entrants to compete effectively, differentiation is more important than ever to earn a sliver of the market.

New companies looking to enter the ultra-healthy quick-service industry may consider pricing their meals high in order break into the market with a premium position, both boosting brand perception and the perception of QSRs. Unfortunately, a new company cannot operate on economies of scale; therefore, it must capitalize on its value proposition and look to break even in other ways. The startup stage requires immense dedication from employees as losses are almost guaranteed.

As Konig discussed Swizzler's pricing, he stated that the "price is premium, but [they] do look to keep it in reason." This high pricing builds a persona around a company and helps build the brand, however. With higher prices, consumers often relate this to higher overall quality. Therefore, consumers may be willing to pay the higher price to receive a meal they trust.

Returning to Tesla, if its first car had not launched eco-friendly transportation as a premium standard, then the brand may have lacked the aura that Elon Musk created around the company. In a similar manner, Swizzler has worked to position itself on the premium side of the market.

While producing high-quality beef franks, it can elevate itself above the mystery meat opponent.

Change within the food industry is surely happening, but not overnight. It is easier to reason through spending top dollar on an elaborate meal, but not so simple when the food doesn't exceed your standards. It's also difficult to spend more money on a meal when you can buy a burger for just about a dollar right next door.

This scenario slowly walks us through unmarked territory, however. Where do we go from here? How is food revolutionized? What will food look like in the future?

By entering the market at this high-end price, as many QSRs have, the value perceived by the customer is much greater than entering at a low price. While costs may be slightly higher than industry averages, the overall margin per product can be exponentially greater than the additional costs. This is because higher quality food brings certain customers additional value and, from here, the restaurant can increase its bottom line.

To rightfully integrate a successful pricing strategy, however, restaurant leadership must understand where the company falls within the market, and where the company should be. Pricing strategies, like many other things, can become extremely complex. This is especially true when earning limited margins on products in the food industry.

Overall, operations must effectively work with a company's strategy. The food industry landscape is slowly changing, and a tactical pricing strategy is just one action moving the industry in a new direction. Through compiling tactical actions, the food industry will slowly evolve, and a new wave of QSR startups can establish their positions within the industry.

VISIONARY LEADERSHIP

With the daunting task of pushing the food industry in a new direction, a great leader must take charge. Taking one leader specifically, we will look at Ron Shaich's influence.

Shaich "is the founder and chairman of Panera Bread, a groundbreaking restaurant brand that today has more than 2,360 bakery-cafes, over 100,000 associates and nearly $6 billion in annual system wide sales," according to the Panera website.[119] With Panera Bread's revolutionary operations, Shaich has shown his ability to influence the future of food in the United States and lead the charge.

---

119 "Management Bios." 2019. *Panera Bread.* https://www.panera-bread.com/en-us/company/about-panera/management-bios.html.

With a bachelor's degree from Clark University, and a master's in business administration from Harvard Business School, Shaich has been a legend in the restaurant industry with awards from the Yale School of Management, the *Nation's Restaurant News*, the IFMA, and Ernst & Young.[120] Shaich has been a major influencer in the way we eat food in America today.

And he has continued to disrupt industries. His action to combine a typical bakery with a café launched the bakery-café market that has taken off. Shaich launched this initiative through Au Bon Pain, eventually selling the restaurant to focus on the success of Panera.[121] By reevaluating the customer experience, Shaich has managed to reinvent certain aspects of the quick-service industry.

While a visionary in the field, Shaich has taken simple gambles throughout his career. He called these actions "smart, long-term bets."[122] These have shifted the company to a different method of restauranteering altogether and, according to Panera, this approach "came to be known as 'fast-casual'—now a $40 billion segment of the restaurant industry."[123]

---

120 Ibid
121 Ibid
122 Ibid
123 Ibid

Shaich's leadership has clearly worked its way down the corporate ladder and branched out into the rest of the food industry. Panera has branched away from the typical, unhealthy fast food market and instead continued to expand into clean, healthy options.

Pushing the company forward, Shaich has acted on key initiatives to give Panera a competitive edge. "The themes [Shaich] bet on — digital, clean, loyalty and omni-channel — are reshaping the restaurant landscape as others race to adopt them, and Panera is leading in all of them," the website describes.[124] Acting on the clear values that Panera's consumers hold dear has allowed Panera to thrive.

Beyond his influence at Panera, however, Shaich has also been extremely influential in other regards. With a strong interest in nonprofits aimed at fixing the food industry, Shaich has had a major role in helping others, especially through his focus on food insecurity issues.

"Ron is also a co-founder of No Labels, an organization that promotes bipartisan political problem solving and the development of a long-term strategic plan for the country," the Panera website adds.[125]

---

124 Ibid
125 Ibid

These actions show that business leaders can influence change outside of standard business operations. This influence can be used for great societal initiatives, as Shaich has clearly shown. Great leaders cannot simply be leaders within their company; they must look to lead the charge and make a change worldwide. Shaich has stepped outside the realm of Panera to help better the world as a whole.

Starting with an idea, then leading Panera Bread to where it is today, Shaich has been just one visionary moving the food industry forward. He is merely one of the many. There are always visionaries looking to enact change. And there is always a leader behind a great initiative.

Visionaries such as Ron Shaich, Elon Musk, Ray Kroc, and even teams within an organization really do have the power to create a lasting impact. And this doesn't strictly pertain to the food industry—any visionary may launch an initiative that may alter the world as we know it. With this, there should always be a desire to innovate and push society forward.

INNOVATIVE, FORWARD THINKING

Ron Shaich understands the competitive nature that a quick service restaurant's face every day.

"In this space, there's only one thing that matters and that is competitive advantage — being a place where people want to walk past your competitors to come in," Shaich stated.[126]

There is fierce competition to steal customers from competitors. Therefore, finding a niche is necessary when entering the market. While operating in the QSR market, Panera has been extremely successful.

"Panera has always had a great management team (and) consistently serves quality and sustainable menu offerings in a homey atmosphere, everything the competition should be doing," said Janet Lowder, president of consultants Restaurant Management Services.[127] The management team at Panera stands as one key component of successful operations; however, the ability to serve consistent quality with a sustainable menu is the voice of the future.

Consumer preferences have shifted toward sustainable operations. Environmental sustainability, nutritional sustainability, and firm sustainability all matter when creating an enticing menu for a startup QSR. By operating through sustainable methods, companies should, in theory, attract consumers

126 Meyer, Zlati, and Charisse Jones. "How Panera Won the Restaurant Game." *USA Today.* April 06, 2017. Accessed April 07, 2019. https://www.usatoday.com/story/money/business/2017/04/06/how-panera-won-restaurant-game/100072546/.

127 Ibid

for the long term as opposed to shorter, more random visits. And when operating a QSR, pleasing repeat customers and retaining these individuals can go much further than attempting to find new customers.

As for consistency, offering a unique product that has been standardized among all store locations allows for the brand image to shine through. A Panera sandwich should be differentiated from a McDonald's cheeseburger, but every time a sandwich is ordered, it should be made exactly the same at all Panera locations. This consistency allows for consumers to know exactly what they are getting when they are ordering at the counter, or nowadays, online.

MANAGING THE STORM

Companies are continuing to advance their technology in all industries. Technological advancements have certainly impacted QSRs. Innovation can be extremely diverse, especially as companies find new ways to add value through investments in technology.

"It's the technology piece of the business which has really taken Panera to a different level," said Bob Derrington, senior research analysist at Telesy Advisory Group. "They can serve consumers well and keep them coming back."[128] By adapting to the market and pinpointing what the consumer wants, Panera Bread has been able to make the most of the technology opportunities.

Innovation will continue to weave its way into food operations. Technology can be implemented to better serve customers and elevate their experience or help the restaurant's profitability. Integration of technological advancements behind the scenes can help craft higher quality initiatives. This can be accomplished through big data analytics and continued research.

With such a great opportunity to build ease and expedite processes, technology allows firms to streamline operations and better serve the customer. By combining the current trends with the age-old activity of eating, new QSRs should be able to roll out stronger business strategies and capture the market by storm. Innovation allows all this to be possible.

* * *

It is evident that all entrepreneurial ventures must journey through many decisions. However, in order to be a successful QSR startup, captivating a loyal audience and building

---

128 Ibid

meaningful relationships is practically a necessity. Through a strategic customer-centric focus, quality relationships can be made.

Who is our customer and what do they want? What do fast food and fast-casual dining look like in a given location? How should we price? Is that too high? Too low? How does the future here look? Who are we and what do we do? Fully understanding where a company would stand in the food industry may allow an entrepreneur to find an untapped niche in the market.

By leveraging the changing perception of fast food, knowing that it's a marathon ahead, having someone lead the charge, and using innovative, forward thinking, companies are able to maneuver themselves through the storm that is the food industry. This book is just a microscopic look at factors that a startup should be aware of.

Innovation and forward thinking then come from the entrepreneurial mindset and the American dream. By working hard, and continuing to learn, an entrepreneur can do their part to make a real difference. The more you know, the better you can manage a company today and in the future. By brainstorming different strategic initiatives, companies can stumble upon luck-stricken opportunities—those that may change the world forever. These few aspects of the journey ahead can hopefully be used to guide the conversation.

CHAPTER TWELVE

CONCLUSION

———

Restaurants now and in the future will have to deal with an ever-changing industry. Trends such as health, diversity, safety, convenience, and social consciousness will shift the industry dynamic moving forward. These trends will add excitement and opportunity into the market.

* * *

Currently, fast food is branded as cheap, a mystery, and unhealthy. However, as we have seen, efforts are being made to alter this common classification. As mentioned time and time again, food is changing, and we are evolving. Our view of how to eat and how to live our lives has dramatically changed in recent years. People are looking for new ways to be successful. This success-driven mindset has always been with us, though—just look at the American dream. We are all on the same quest.

That said, however, health isn't something that everyone really cares about. People still drink, smoke, and eat unhealthily despite all the information out there to suggest they shouldn't. The success of these newer ultra-health-focused QSRs will be run for those looking to be healthy, which isn't everyone. Because of this, these companies must tailor their focus specifically to those looking for a healthier lifestyle.

People looking for a change will connect closely with this message, while others will simply fall out of the targeted segment of consumers. Not everyone will fall into this demographic, but there are always people grinding for a better lifestyle. These are the ones who will truly value this message.

Food currently does not have the connotation of being fuel for success. But moving forward, this idea will grow. Those looking to achieve goals will eat healthy, work hard, and exercise; from here, things will begin to fall into place. Food in the future will be a great factor for overall life success.

While ideally everyone would view what they eat as a means for achieving success, the actual implications of something like this go far behind changes of just one industry. In general, the staple unhealthy food system we live with today will always be a part of our life. People are not suddenly going to shift their preferences toward salads over pizza and ice cream, for example. But there *will* be a greater emphasis on eating healthy food moving forward.

Society at large has a major stake in the QSR industry, and in this new era of restaurants, things are going to look a whole lot different.

For this to happen, however, society must value the status of being healthy. Health, above all else, must be branded as an achievement that someone can obtain. Reaching the healthy benchmark should be tied in with overall life success, like love, money, and happiness are currently. By promoting this journey to success, eating healthy will become a necessary stepping stone to achieving goals.

The actual benefits must be proven as well, but this will only occur through education.

This education goes beyond QSRs: customers must understand the implications of eating a well-balanced meal for their body. Furthermore, they should understand that their entire life can evolve simply from the food they put into their body. No longer will watching what you eat mean just counting calories; instead, food will become the fuel for the mind and body.

However, as stated before, there are many opportunities present in the food industry, and an entrepreneur has the choice to create as they wish.

From the opportunities present, however, there will be new entrants. Instead of cheap, unhealthy meals, new players are likely to enter the market with unique, healthy offerings. In due time, people nationwide will look to be healthy, even more than they already do. However, major industry dynamics are not altered overnight, as we looked at; it takes a marathon to make it all happen. For new and existing restaurants, patience is key.

* * *

Regarding operations, food will ideally be branded with immense clarity throughout the entire supply-chain process. Consumers should be able to understand where their food comes from and how it transitions from farm to table. This transparency in the supply chain has recently been receiving coverage as new firms look to empower everyone along the production line. In an ever-increasing world of collaboration and communication, the relationships that these firms are able to create add value for all stakeholders.

As you may have noticed by now, restaurants are part of a complex industry. Consumers only complicate it further;

however, by thinking through various perspectives, an entrepreneur can craft a unique strategy. For example, each year, New Year's marks the time when resolutions are made. People quickly look to get their life on track and eat healthy for the new year. A startup tied with life success will thrive during this time. Unfortunately for many customers, however, they fall out of these good habits after some time.

Individuals across the United States make certain life goals at various times, thus those looking to better themselves may seek out an ultra-health establishment for assistance. For a company to successfully operate here, it must hook customers and keep them coming back. The cost of acquiring new customers is often large, so if a QSR can keep a steady base of consumers, it'll have much steadier operations.

Even with this, however, customers are likely to go through different phases of motivation. Customers may go through a cycle when they are highly motivated and seek out healthy food at all times, but then they may also reach periods where they lose all interest.

This cycle is evidently seen around New Year's. We have all seen the super crowded gym right after the strike of the new year. But this enthusiasm slowly tapers off as people begin to break their New Year's resolutions.

Following this, though, customers may spontaneously stop in as they are still looking to be healthy every so often. This is true with both healthy restaurants and gyms. While revenue earned may slump during slow periods, other customers are likely motivated and determined to make a change.

Consumers will begin to strive for success by working out, eating healthy, and working hard. As an ultra-health QSR entrepreneur, it is then *your* job to illustrate the value they will receive by purchasing *your* healthy food. The link between success and your brand is vital.

Moreover, there is an opportunity present within the marketplace currently. People are looking to achieve success and make a difference in the world, and food is one way of getting there.

* * *

The future of food will lead to a difference in the world. This takes shape in many different ways.

Acting under strong ethical principles regarding food practices can lead companies to operate with sustainable methods. Firms certainly need to operate under a sustainable cash model—allowing more money to come in than go out—but there is more to business than just money.

When we look at the bigger picture, we see there are actions that must be taken. Environmental sustainability efforts can be implemented to help protect the earth. These actions have gained major traction, especially lately. When firms engage in eco-friendly activities, they can decrease their overall footprint.

The estimated cost of catastrophe due to the climate crisis is a major force we face living on Earth. Because of this, younger generations have formed many core values based on the understanding of this issue. Since the possible effects of a climate disaster play such a large role in the lives of people around the world, QSRs must do their job to limit destruction.

Agriculture and food production have the ability to swing climate change effects. Food consumption and sourcing can make a huge difference in the outcome of our planet. So, by individually operating with a socially conscious ideology, the large-scale disaster caused by mankind may be limited.

* * *

As consumers push for healthy, diverse, safe, convenient, and socially conscious practices, restaurants will increasingly work to accommodate their desires. Younger generations hold a certain ideology about the world we live in. We—as a twenty-year-old myself—have an idea on how things should be run. In this situation, as we grow up, changes will be made that will rock the industry and the world for decades.

Therefore, for those looking to make an impact in the everyday life of Americans, food is the way to go. A strive for an entrepreneurial venture will push society forward as the general public advances its views on the benefits of food.

The old saying states that "*my body is a temple*," but soon people will use this framework as the foundation of their successes. Food will build the body and the mind, and from there, anything will become possible.

The alterations to society's perception on food must undergo a marathon of change before any great impact is seen, however. As change in any industry is inevitable, the battle to instill a new ideology of success branded food into society will not occur overnight. But these alterations are quickly being incorporated now.

New trends, new diets, new restaurants, more variety, and extreme specialty exhibit the changes being made to the food industry today. Change is happening everywhere, and soon, it will outweigh the old perspective we hold regarding fast food. No longer are the days of unhealthy foods. Instead, the future of food holds health and quality above all else.

The future of food is bright. There are many positive aspects influencing QSRs. As we go forth, I hope for society to evolve and accommodate the necessary adjustments to everyday life to allow these health-focused QSRs to thrive. By pushing the success-driven mindset forward, American ideals may be further intertwined with the basic function of eating. As this occurs, food will be forever changed for the better.

Food has a variety of places it may go. However, in reality, it will go wherever we want it to go. Therefore, by understanding the values we hold dear to us, we can understand the future of food. Consumers will internalize the additional value their small contribution has to our planet. From here, we change the world. One step at a time, we learn to innovate food fast.

ACKNOWLEDGEMENTS

———

I would first like to thank all those who have contributed their expert knowledge to the creation of this book. Without these many individuals, I would not have been able to fully understand the complex inner-workings of the food industry. With many stories, both referenced and referenced anonymously, I would like to specifically acknowledge the insights and experiences that many individuals have generously shared with me. These stories have added to the success of this publication and have significantly improved my journey. I thank you all.

I would also like to thank those that have helped contribute to both the writing and publication processes. Every step of the way, I have been lucky enough to have colleagues, editors, and many others help out. My journey has always been a team effort.

Furthermore, I'd like to thank everyone else who has supported me in the creation of this book. The names are as follows; however, their continuous support deserves much more than just recognition: Jim & Andi Heidenreich, Luke Heidenreich, Zach Heidenreich, Gary & Fran Heidenreich, Melva & John Richards, Tony & Rachel Vecchio, Gerald & Eva Heidenreich, Canon Heidenreich, Kris & John Widmann, Nick Widmann, Ben Widmann, Eric Koester, Dave Lumley, Mary Kaffenberger, Elizabeth Kaffenberger, Hannah Donahue, Logan Maier, Lynne & Roger Mills, Tyna Swatek, Diane & James Jellison, Jennifer McArthur & Sach Jogal, Leanne & Scott Riggs, Jeanine & Dale Johanning, Mike Welch & Susannah Carter Welch, Luke Palmer, Luke Stangl, Brooke Blythe, Mimi Ramsbottom, YoYo Ghannam, Charlie Cronkright, Kimberly Ng, Yanan Wang, Joseph Ready, Tristan Rhee, Danny Maher, Joshua Moscato, Brad Silver, Jacob Arnold, and Nathan Martin. Without these individuals, the journey would be impossible.

WORKS CITED

CHAPTER ONE:

"Adult Obesity Facts | Overweight & Obesity | CDC." *Centers for Disease Control and Prevention.* Accessed April 07, 2019. https://www.cdc.gov/obesity/data/adult.html.

Farfan, Barbara. "Quotes From McDonald's Visonary Ray Kroc About Building a Brand." *The Balance Small Business.* Accessed April 07, 2019. https://www.thebalancesmb.com/mcdonalds-ray-kroc-quotes-2892155.

"Fast Food: U.S. Growth Industry." *CQ Researcher.* Accessed March 22, 2019. https://library.cqpress.com/cqresearcher/document.php?id=cqresrre1978120800.

McGrath, Maggie. "Why $200 Million Will Make Sweetgreen The Next Big Thing In Delivery (And, Yes, A Unicorn)." *Forbes*. November 13, 2018. Accessed April 07, 2019. https://www.forbes.com/sites/maggiemcgrath/2018/11/13/the-salad-unicorn-how-sweetgreens-200-million-capital-infusion-will-propel-the-chain-to-new-heights/#152ce24d3acc.

Murray, Rheana. "Fast Food Burgers Have Tripled in Size since the 1950s: CDC graphic." *Nydailynews.com*. January 10, 2019. Accessed March 22, 2019. https://www.nydailynews.com/life-style/health/fast-food-burgers-tripled-size-1950s-cdc-graphic-article-1.1083573.

Police, Sara. "How Much Have Obesity Rates Risen Since 1950?" *LIVESTRONG.COM*. Accessed March 22, 2019. https://www.livestrong.com/article/384722-how-much-have-obesity-rates-risen-since-1950/.

Rosenberg, Matt. "How Many McDonald's Restaurants Operate Worldwide?" *ThoughtCo.* January 25, 2019. Accessed April 07, 2019. https://www.thoughtco.com/number-of-mcdonalds-restaurants-worldwide-1435174.

CHAPTER TWO:

Drive-in Restaurant. Accessed March 30, 2019. http://umich.edu/~drivein/restaurant.html.

"FAST FOOD: The Fast Lane of Life [MODERN MARVELS
FULL DOCUMENTARY}." YouTube video, 44:02. "Documentaries Unlimited," February 26, 2014. https://youtu.
be/BPf22nRVy2I.

"The New Definition of "Fast Food". *QSR Magazine.* April 19,
2010. Accessed April 07, 2019. https://www.qsrmagazine.
com/news/new-definition-fast-food.

"QSR." *Urban Dictionary.* Accessed April 07, 2019. https://
www.urbandictionary.com/define.php?term=QSR.

CHAPTER THREE:

"Adult Obesity Facts | Overweight & Obesity | CDC." *Centers
for Disease Control and Prevention.* Accessed April 07,
2019. https://www.cdc.gov/obesity/data/adult.html.

Meyer, Zlati, and Charisse Jones. "How Panera Won the
Restaurant Game." *USA Today.* April 06, 2017. Accessed
April 07, 2019. https://www.usatoday.com/story/money/
business/2017/04/06/how-panera-won-restaurant-
game/100072546/.

"Our History: Ray Kroc & The McDonald's Brothers | McDon-
ald's." Our History: Ray Kroc & The McDonald's Broth-

ers | McDonald's. Accessed April 07, 2019. https://www.
mcdonalds.com/us/en-us/about-us/our-history.html.

"Public Views About Americans' Eating Habits." *Pew Research
Center Science & Society.* December 1, 2016. Accessed June
14, 2019. https://www.pewresearch.org/science/2016/12/01/
public-views-about-americans-eating-habits/.

"Ray Kroc Quotes." *BrainyQuote.* Accessed May 29, 2019.
https://www.brainyquote.com/quotes/ray_kroc_173417.

"We Are Panera Bread." *Panera Bread.* Accessed April 7, 2019.
https://www.panerabread.com/en-us/company/about-
panera.html.

CHAPTER FOUR:

"Dietary Guidelines." *Office of Disease Prevention and Health
Promotion.* March 11, 2019. Accessed April 07, 2019. https://
health.gov/dietaryguidelines/.

"Food as Fuel Before, During and After Workouts." *American
Heart Association.* January 2, 2015. https://www.heart.org/
en/healthy-living/healthy-eating/eat-smart/nutrition-ba-
sics/food-as-fuel-before-during-and-after-workouts.

Selhub, Eva. 2018. "Nutritional Psychiatry: Your Brain on Food." *Harvard Health Blog.* April 5, 2018. https://www.health.harvard.edu/blog/nutritional-psychiatry-your-brain-on-food-201511168626.

CHAPTER FIVE:

"2018 Festival Keynote - Tony Shure, Chopt - Founder Story & Problem Solution Fit." YouTube video, 3:00. "NYU Entrepreneurial Institute (Leslie eLab)," April 19, 2018. https://youtu.be/cgKqJEGFSXM.

"About Us." *Juice Press.* Accessed April 07, 2019. https://juice-press.com/about-us/.

Baer, Drake. "This Trendy Salad Bar's Design Secrets Keep Customers Coming Back for More." *Business Insider.* March 21, 2016. Accessed April 07, 2019. https://www.businessinsider.com/sweetgreen-founder-interview-nathaniel-ru-2016-3.

Bertoni, Steven. "PODCAST: Sweetgreen Cofounder Jonathan Neman On Turning Salad Into A Lifestyle." *Forbes.* July 24, 2018. Accessed April 07, 2019. https://www.forbes.com/sites/stevenbertoni/2018/07/24/podcast-sweetgreen-cofounder-jonathan-neman-on-turning-salad-into-a-lifestyle/#1738d9001766.

"Best Diets Overall." *U.S. News & World Report.* Accessed April 07, 2019. https://health.usnews.com/best-diet/mediterranean-diet.

Clifford, Catherine. "Dig Inn Founder: 'I Wouldn't Let People Tell You That You Can't Do Things'." *Entrepreneur.* September 26, 2014. Accessed April 07, 2019. https://www.entrepreneur.com/video/237836.

"Fast Food Revolution | Adam Eskin | TEDxBinghamton-University." YouTube video, 18:08. "TEDx Talks," March 27, 2015. https://youtu.be/NMT7ulSKxog?list=PL4ax-zonXAvkyjwepMfoI8sn1g1jy2pWx3.

Garrity, Philip. "Get To Know Chop't Creative Salad Company's CEO Nick Marsh." *INC.* Accessed April 07, 2019. http://www.westchestermagazine.com/914-INC/Q4-2014/Get-To-Know-Chopt-Creative-Salad-Companys-CEO-Nick-Marsh/.

"How Sweetgreen's Co-Founders Are Creating a New Model for Fast Food." *Fortune.* Accessed April 07, 2019. http://fortune.com/2016/02/18/sweetgreen-entrepreneurs/.

"Interview with Marcus Antebi - Founder of Juice Press." YouTube video, 5:34. "New to the Street," November 20, 2014. https://youtu.be/ksCIqAKGBUY.

Johnson, Eric. "Why Sweetgreen Thinks like a Tech Company." *Recode*. December 17, 2018. Accessed April 07, 2019. https://www.recode.net/2018/12/17/18144250/sweetgreen-jonathan-neman-fast-food-salad-delivery-blockchain-kara-swisher-decode-podcast.

Kowitt, Beth. "How Sweetgreen's Co-Founders Are Creating a New Model for Fast Food." *Fortune*. February 18, 2016. Accessed April 07, 2019. http://fortune.com/2016/02/18/sweetgreen-entrepreneurs/.

"McDonald's Reports Fourth Quarter And Full Year 2018 Results And Quarterly Cash Dividend." *McDonald's Corporation*. Accessed May 2, 2019. https://news.mcdonalds.com/news-releases/news-release-details/mcdonalds-reports-fourth-quarter-and-full-year-2018-results-and.

Minehan, Katie. "Marcus Antebi - Juice Press Founder Interview." Marcus Antebi - Juice Press Founder Interview. March 8, 2014. Accessed April 07, 2019. https://www.refinery29.com/en-us/marcus-antebi-juice-press.

"Our Mission." *Dig Inn*. Accessed April 07, 2019. https://www.diginn.com/mission/.

"Our Story." *Sweetgreen*. Accessed April 07, 2019. https://www.sweetgreen.com/our-story/.

Paul, Eve Turow. "Dig Inn Slows Down Its Quick Service Model." *Forbes.* January 11, 2017. Accessed April 07, 2019. https://www.forbes.com/sites/eveturowpaul/2017/01/11/dig-inn-runs-from-quick-service/#580051b51684.

"Resolutions Done Right." *Zoës Kitchen.* Accessed April 07, 2019. https://zoeskitchen.com/.

Ruggless, Ron. "Zoe's Kitchen Debuts Next-generation Design." *Nation's Restaurant News.* January 16, 2018. Accessed April 07, 2019. https://www.nrn.com/marketing/zoe-s-kitchen-debuts-next-generation-design.

"Vulnerability Is the New Black | Adam Eskin | Change Food Fest." YouTube video, 8:09. "Change Food," December 23, 2016. https://youtu.be/8Qwx3IToOpg.

"What's Different about Zoës Kitchen." *CNBC.* September 02, 2014. Accessed April 07, 2019. https://www.cnbc.com/video/2014/09/02/whats-different-about-zos-kitchen.html?&qsearchterm=ZOES.

"What Inspires Chopt CEO Nick Marsh." *QSR Magazine.* January 13, 2017. Accessed April 07, 2019. https://www.qsrmagazine.com/start-finish-what-inspires-execs/what-inspires-chopt-ceo-nick-marsh.

"Zoe's Kitchen CEO: Differentiated Brand." *CNBC*. May 18, 2015. Accessed April 07, 2019. https://www.cnbc.com/video/2015/05/18/zoes-kitchen-ceo-differentiated-brand-.html.

CHAPTER SIX:

Carrington, Damian. 2018. "Avoiding Meat and Dairy Is 'Single Biggest Way' to Reduce Your Impact on Earth." *The Guardian*. May 31, 2018. https://www.theguardian.com/environment/2018/may/31/avoiding-meat-and-dairy-is-single-biggest-way-to-reduce-your-impact-on-earth.

Klein, Danny. "By Chloe Looks to Double Footprint After $31M Investment." *QSR Magazine*. April 05, 2018. Accessed April 07, 2019. https://www.qsrmagazine.com/fast-casual/chloe-looks-double-footprint-after-31m-investment.

"Redefining What It Means to Eat Well | the Story." *By CHLOE*. Accessed April 07, 2019. https://eatbychloe.com/the-story/.

Settembre, Jeanette. "EXCLUSIVE: By CHLOE, the Vegan Shake Shack, Receives $31 Million Investment to Expand Globally." *MarketWatch*. April 05, 2018. Accessed April 07, 2019. https://www.marketwatch.com/story/exclusive-by-

chloe-the-vegan-shake-shack-receives-31-million-invest-
ment-to-expand-globally-2018-04-05-8882611.

"The Hidden Costs of Hamburgers." *PBS*. Public Broadcasting
Service. August 2, 2012. Accessed March 22, 2019. https://
www.pbs.org/newshour/science/the-hidden-costs-of-
hamburgers.

Wasser, Samantha. "How a Partner Behind the Famous
Vegan Restaurant Chain By Chloe Moved Forward After
a Lawsuit, Online Harassment and a Miscarriage." *Entrepreneur*. August 29, 2018. Accessed April 07, 2019. https://
www.entrepreneur.com/article/318862.

CHAPTER SEVEN:

"Food Safety Home Page | CDC." *Centers for Disease Control
and Prevention*. Accessed May 24, 2019. https://www.cdc.
gov/foodsafety/index.html.

CHAPTER EIGHT:

Hirschberg, Carsten, Alexander Rajko, Thomas Schum-
acher, and Martin Wrulich. "The Changing Market for
Food Delivery." *McKinsey & Company*. November 2016.
Accessed May 24, 2019. https://www.mckinsey.com/

industries/high-tech/our-insights/the-changing-market-for-food-delivery.

"How Far Does Your Food Travel to Get to Your Plate?" *CUESA*. February 5, 2018. Accessed May 24, 2019. https://cuesa.org/learn/how-far-does-your-food-travel-get-your-plate.

Zaleski, Olivia. "Restaurants Shrink as Food Delivery Apps Get More Popular." *Bloomberg*. October 29, 2018. https://www.bloomberg.com/news/articles/2018-10-29/restaurants-shrink-as-food-delivery-apps-get-more-popular.

Zion, Aric, Fred Petrovsky, Jennifer Spangler, and Thomas Hollman. "Food Delivery Apps: Usage and Demographics - Winners, Losers and Laggards." *Zion and Zion*. Accessed May 24, 2019. https://www.zionandzion.com/research/food-delivery-apps-usage-and-demographics-winners-losers-and-laggards/.

CHAPTER NINE:

Carrington, Damian. 2018. "Avoiding Meat and Dairy Is 'Single Biggest Way' to Reduce Your Impact on Earth." *The Guardian*. May 31, 2018. https://www.theguardian.com/environment/2018/may/31/avoiding-meat-and-dairy-is-single-biggest-way-to-reduce-your-impact-on-earth.

Mills, Eliza. "Veggie Grill CEO Steve Heeley on Expansion and 'veggie Positivity'." *Marketplace*. January 6, 2017. Accessed April 07, 2019. https://www.marketplace.org/2017/01/06/business/veggie-grill-ceo-steve-heeley-expansion-and-veggie-positivity.

"We See Veggies For What They Are." *Veggie Grill*. Accessed April 07, 2019. https://www.veggiegrill.com/our-story.html.

CHAPTER TEN:

Matousek, Mark. "Elon Musk Says People Need To Work Around 80 Hours Per Week To Change The World." *Business Insider*. November 26, 2018. Accessed June 14, 2019. https://www.businessinsider.com/elon-musk-says-80-hours-per-week-needed-change-the-world-2018-11.

"Ray Kroc Quotes." *BrainyQuote*. Xplore. Accessed May 24, 2019. https://www.brainyquote.com/quotes/ray_kroc_173414.

CHAPTER ELEVEN:

"Management Bios." 2019. *Panera Bread*. https://www.panerabread.com/en-us/company/about-panera/management-bios.html.

Meyer, Zlati, and Charisse Jones. "How Panera Won the Restaurant Game." *USA Today*. April 06, 2017. Accessed April 07, 2019. https://www.usatoday.com/story/money/business/2017/04/06/how-panera-won-restaurant-game/100072546/.

CHAPTER TWELVE:

None.

www.ingramcontent.com/pod-product-compliance
Lightning Source LLC
Chambersburg PA
CBHW071522180526
45171CB00002B/350